CHASED
Alone, Black, and Undercover

CHASED

Alone, Black, and Undercover

Billy Chase and
Lennie Grimaldi

NEW HORIZON PRESS   *Far Hills, New Jersey*

Copyright © 1994 by Billy Chase and Lennie Grimaldi

All rights reserved. No portion of this book may be reproduced or transmitted in any form whatsoever, including electronic, mechanical, or any information storage or retrieval system, except as may be expressly permitted in the 1976 Copyright Act.

Requests for permission should be addressed to:
New Horizon Press
P.O. Box 669
Far Hills, NJ 07931

Chase, Billy, and Lennie Grimaldi.
    Chased : Alone, black, and undercover

Library of Congress Catalog Card Number: 93-84522

ISBN: 0-88282-077-X
New Horizon Press

Manufactured in the U.S.A.

1997 1996 1995 1994 1993 / 5 4 3 2 1

DEDICATION

To the children of
Sammy E. Cohen Middle School, Atlanta, Georgia,
and my love, Rita

—B.C.

To J.A.P.

—L.G.

ACKNOWLEDGMENTS

The authors would like to thank the following individuals for their insight, support, and assistance in the preparation of this book:

The staff at New Horizon Press; *Connecticut Post* reporters Richard Peck, Michael Daly, Michael Mayko, and John Gilmore; James Callahan; Stanley Twardy; Ron Bailey; Don Cathey; Ruben Bradford; Jack Flynn; Jerome Spates; family, friends, and co-workers.

CONTENTS

: Prologue : 1
1 : Barnumtown : 5
2 : Early Chase : 11
3 : Corrections : 23
4 : The Connecticut Crew : 33
5 : Ebony and Ivory : 41
6 : Bridgeport PD : 51
7 : Fort Dicks : 67
8 : Sewers : 79
9 : The Number One Family : 85
10 : Broken Family : 97
11 : Cats and Rats : 111
12 : Sorry, Ma : 125
13 : Rich Druggies, Poor Druggies : 135
14 : Crack Heads, Crack Fights : 143
15 : Workaholic : 151
16 : Mob Ties : 157
17 : "The Boys" : 167
18 : Who Killed Tommy DeBrizzi? : 177
19 : The Setup : 183
20 : The Color of Law Enforcement : 189
21 : Death Notices : 195
22 : Torture : 203
23 : Train Wreck : 209
24 : The Final Days : 219
25 : Retirement : 225

AUTHORS' NOTE

These are true experiences. The personalities, events, actions, and conversations portrayed within the story have been reconstructed from extensive interviews and research, utilizing court documents, letters, personal papers, press accounts, and the memories of participants. In an effort to safeguard the privacy of certain individuals, the authors have changed their names and, in some cases, altered otherwise identifying characteristics. Events involving the characters happened as described; only minor details have been altered.

Prologue

LATE ONE CALM autumn afternoon in 1989, Billy Chase had a feeling that something wasn't quite right.

It was the intuitive feeling he had often in his maddeningly bizarre life, a life of aliases, paranoia, and danger, the life of an unusual undercover cop.

In his short, dizzying career, Chase made a habit of collecting enemies, plenty of them—and he hadn't even reached his thirty-first birthday.

When you take away five or ten years from the lives of utterly ruthless people struggling for power, you are not as easily forgotten as, say, a piece of gum stuck to the bottom of a shoe. Chase, the gumshoe, bothered people, especially criminals.

Returning home from another day investigating drug gangs,

crack heads, and Mafia hitmen, he drove his gray 1986 BMW into the garage of the brick-built condominium complex that was his home in a quiet neighborhood in Bridgeport, Connecticut, a tough working-class city roughly sixty miles from New York City. Bridgeport's streets featured names of U.S. Presidents such as Lincoln and McKinley, men who knew something about acquiring enemies themselves.

Exceptionally handsome, six-feet four-inches tall, a wiry 185 pounds, wearing a short sleeve tan polo shirt with the right insignia, perfectly frayed blue jeans, and designer sun glasses, Chase exited the Beamer, on loan from the Connecticut State Police. The car and his appearance provided his cover. Chase investigated drug dealers, so he did everything he could to look like one. Even if the BMW wasn't new, it was close enough with its fancy sports coupe look, telephone, and high-tech stereo thumping Chase's favorite rap artist, Kool Moe Dee. Entering the side door of the condo complex, his stomach growled, demanding some attention. Chase reached into the refrigerator, grabbed a ham and provolone sandwich, his favorite, and headed across the street to see Joe Simpson, a neighbor.

Biting into his sandwich, he crossed Taft Avenue; the sight of a beige Toyota with tinted windows idling on the wrong side of the street caught his eye. Maybe, he thought to himself, the driver was lost or was waiting on a girlfriend.

Returning home after a brief visit, Chase observed that the car had pulled closer, still on the wrong side of the street. Cautiously, he placed his hand inside of his jacket, feeling for the 9-millimeter Smith & Wesson. He entered his apartment, still feeling uneasy. Normally, he'd have put the lights on. But just in case someone was planning to give him a dark surprise, he decided to leave them off so he could adjust his eyes.

Stealthily he approached the living room window and cracked the shade. His visitors didn't bother to knock. A blizzard of bullets zoomed toward Chase's head from the street, reverberating off the

CHASED

front of the brick condominium unit. The second volley from the semi-automatic weapon exploded as Chase crash-landed to the floor. His heart pumped like a piston, his mind raced with fear, then anger. Chase pulled out his gun, but it was too late. The car screeched away.

Flat on the floor, all alone, he felt a sick despair in the pit of his stomach. He thought about his children and then the insanity gripping his life. This was the very reason the mothers of his children kept his kids away from him.

"It's a good thing they don't know how to shoot straight," Chase muttered to himself, by way of reality, or relief.

Some undercover cops have an immediate idea about who needs them out of the way. Chase had no such clue. Too many wanted to waste him.

To the ruthless drug dealers draining the city, Chase wasn't just any undercover cop. He grew up in their neighborhoods, lunched with them as schoolmates in high school, and later had the audacity to infiltrate their drug world.

He was the single most dangerous threat to their livelihood.

He was a cop who had taken down major Jamaican drug dealers, Colombian crack lords, and murderous drug gangs terrorizing neighborhoods.

He had gone where few undercovers of his kind had gone before, infiltrating a racketeering operation of the Gambino crime family that was used as the basis of an indictment against the most powerful organized crime figure in the United States, John Gotti.

But Chase wasn't just any undercover squeezing through the cracks of an increasingly clumsy Mafia underworld, a secret society that had succumbed to intensive investigative efforts, major wiretap cases, and stoolies providing information on its inner workings. The kind of news Chase provided was the most unconscionable and embarrassing breach of mob secrecy possible, because Billy Chase was black.

Gotti's gang had allowed a moolinyan—a *tuzzone*, an eggplant, a charcoal, a black man—to dupe them, allowed him to get close enough to put a number of made members and associates of his crew out of business. Nothing could be worse to the psyche of a Mafia hood, except, maybe, his wife sleeping with one.

Who wanted Chase dead?

The list was getting longer than the rap sheets of the criminals he was arresting.

Chase picked up the phone and called the Bridgeport Police Department for help. Ten minutes later Chase's phone rang. On the other end was a friend in the department, Officer Ron Henderson.

"You okay?" Henderson asked.

"Where are you?" Chased replied.

"I'm calling from across the street."

"What are you doing over there?"

"I like you, you're my friend, but there ain't no use for the both of us to get fucked up. You think it's cool to come over now?"

"Thanks a lot. You cops are supposed to protect my ass and even you don't do me any good."

Later that evening in his bed, Chase chilled. Sleepless, his gun at his side, he stared at the television all night and into the morning, listening for passing cars or unannounced guests.

It wasn't the first sleepless night, the first threat against his life, or the first law enforcement official worried that his life was in danger if he got too close to Chase.

In fact, it was the usual . . . for a hero nobody knew about.

CHAPTER 1

Barnumtown

BRIDGEPORT, CONNECTICUT, WAS Phineas Taylor Barnum's adopted city.

Unlike its two older counterparts in the Constitution State, Hartford and New Haven, Bridgeport wasn't incorporated until 1836, when citizens soured on the town's form of government and decided that it needed all the privileges of an incorporated city, including the power to borrow money to build a railroad.

In 1840, the first trains of the Housatonic Railroad Company steamed into Bridgeport Harbor, where shops of every kind filled the downtown, including those advertising women's shawls from Paris and specialty shops dealing exclusively in hats, clothes, and hand-sewn boots. The trains handled freight arriving by ship from the West Indies and American ports such as New York, Philadelphia, Boston, and Baltimore.

Before Barnum gave much thought to such a place as Bridgeport, he was halfway through his life. Barnum was born July 5, 1810, in Bethel, Connecticut, a rural community that shared a border with Danbury, home to a growing hat manufacturing industry. It lay about thirty miles northwest of Bridgeport, along Connecticut's western border with New York State. Here Barnum first tested himself as the world's greatest promoter when he turned his attention to the newspaper business and circulated the first issue of *The Herald of Freedom*, a muckraking sheet that fought "bigotry, superstition, fanaticism and hypocrisy."

Barnum was arrested for libel three times in three years; the third time sent him to jail for sixty days after he accused a Bethel deacon of being "guilty of taking usury of an orphan boy." Barnum's jailing won him the sympathetic praises of the public and mushroomed the popularity of his paper, which continued to publish despite his incarceration. Townspeople threw Barnum a parade upon his release.

Knowing when to quit while ahead, Barnum sold the paper shortly thereafter and moved to New York, where he launched his showman career by hiring an old black woman, Joice Heth, who he claimed was 161 years old and George Washington's former nurse. In New York he convinced a friend to help him purchase the American Museum, filling his showplace with numerous odd attractions, including the Fejee Mermaid (a combination monkey and fish), the Wild Men of Borneo, the bearded lady Josephine Clofullia, and Chang and Eng, the original Siamese twins. Barnum became a national favorite.

Meanwhile, Barnum's greatest attraction, the one that catapulted him to international fame, was growing up in Bridgeport—a twenty-five-inch boy named Charles S. Stratton. Barnum was introduced to Stratton in 1842 by his brother Philo Barnum, who operated a hotel in Bridgeport. After seeing Stratton, Barnum immediately determined that such a remarkably small child should

CHASED

be exhibited in public. Billing him the smallest man alive, Barnum dubbed Stratton "General Tom Thumb" and paraded him before the crowned heads of Europe, including Queen Victoria, and famed leaders closer to home, such as Abraham Lincoln.

Barnum so loved what he saw in Bridgeport that he decided to make it his home; its transportation, waterfront charm, and proximity to New York were just what he wanted.

Barnum saw Bridgeport's potential for growth and took advantage of it. The showman purchased seven hundred acres of land on the city's East Side and created a development plan to lure to Bridgeport both the first industrial establishments and the influx of restless and weary European immigrants willing to work in those factories for cheap pay.

Barnum enticed the inventor of the first working sewing machine, Elias Howe, to open a manufacturing plant that shipped sewing machines around the world. Soon other manufacturers joined: brass, electrical, corset, machine tool, munitions. Bridgeport exploded on the scene as an industrial boomtown, a place where Europeans looked across the sea toward a city that would provide them a job and a new way of life.

Bridgeport also had a genial—if not outright corrupt—nightlife district downtown that by the turn of the Twentieth Century was a place *Bridgeport Herald* reporter Richard Howell called "Bohemia" because watering-hole faithfuls would wander in and out of piano and fiddler music halls. The gin mill hoppers along Water Street would sometimes walk across the street and drop off the dock. "Some were fished out and some drifted out with the tide into Long Island Sound, never to be heard of again," reported Howell.

Though he was long gone, Barnum's developmental influence in Bridgeport continued into the Twentieth Century. The town was built with the sweat and muscle of immigrant groups from throughout Europe. When World War I broke out, the U.S. government capitalized on the city's labor force. In less than a year's time, it built the Remington Arms plant. A marvel of its age, the complex featured thirteen interconnected five-story buildings, the single largest factory building in the world, occupying 77.6 acres.

When Germany invaded Russia at the beginning of World War I, Czar Nicholas II commissioned Remington to produce one million rifles and one hundred million rounds of ammunition for the Imperial Russian Army. The Browning machine gun and Colt automatic pistol were manufactured there. Remington produced seven million rounds of ammunition a week, two-thirds of all ammunition produced in the United States for the Allied cause.

Bridgeport Yankee ingenuity and immigrant might spawned a number of offbeat and progressive firsts. The city was the manufacturing center for Simon Lakes's submarine, Buckminster Fuller's three-wheeled, cucumber-shaped car the Dymaxion, Igor Sikorsky's helicopter, and Columbia Records stars such as Benny Goodman, Gene Autry, and Count Basie.

Bridgeport's reputation for invention even drew the Wham-O Manufacturing Company into the act. Bridgeport was famous for its Frisbie Pies. Yale students in the 1940s loved flinging the heavy metal pie tins on the New Haven Green. Inspired by the sight of Yalies skimming the tins, Wham-O developed its own plastic model, the Frisbee, which has soared through every yard, beach, and park in America.

But the city's motto, *"Industria Crescimus*—By Industry We Thrive," would soon begin to take a drastic turn for the worse: By Industry We Die.

Like may industrial cities, Bridgeport was getting old. Its rundown factories needed repair, its shabby downtown a facelift. More than that, the heyday of the machine tool industry in the 1950s was slowly coming to an end. Japan, which had been bombed into the ground, was forced into building modern facilities and produced casting and aluminum, which cut through the heart of Bridgeport's powerful machine tool industry. Japan's cheaper work force

CHASED

grabbed the basic market in cars, machine tools, and eventually in the electronics industry. In order to cut shipping costs, many Bridgeport companies moved closer to the Midwest, where car makers were located, while others moved south for the luxury of cheaper labor and parent companies closed antiquated Bridgeport plants.

The post–World War II years saw Underwood, Singer, Columbia Records, Bridgeport Brass, Bryant Electric, Remington Arms, and others either relocated or shut down. The industry void chipped away at the city's tax base and severed thousands of jobs held by inner-city residents, paving the way for poverty, despair, and drugs.

This was the inner-city Bridgeport into which Billy Chase was born.

CHAPTER 2

Early Chase

THIRD IN A FAMILY of six children, Billy was raised in the city's North End, where thousands of Italian and Irish immigrants went to escape the despair of their homelands, and increasingly where working- and middle-class blacks fled from the inner-city ghettos.

Billy's mother and father were high school sweethearts reared in Florida. His father, William Joseph Chase Sr., was raised Roman Catholic by his parents, whose bi-racial marriage included a heritage of African American, Seminole, and Cherokee Indian.

Billy's maternal grandfather, born in Ireland, moved to Florida at a young age, where he, a white man, fell for a black woman attending a black high school—something that generated much attention in the segregated south.

"My grandmother didn't like it, but she gave consent for them to get married," says Billy's mom, Nellie. "She said that she'd rather give a nice wedding than to have my parents run off.

"My maternal grandmother told us that she didn't want us standing over someone's pots and pans," she recalls. "I always wanted to be a nurse since I was a little girl. The kids called me Nurse Nellie."

After graduating nursing school in Augusta, Georgia, she encountered persistent ridicule and bigotry at the Florida hospital where she was employed.

"I would be called Nurse Chase," Nellie said. "The caucasian women would be called either Miss or Missus. They ate in beautiful dining rooms; we ate in a maintenance room with wooden tables. We've come a long way today, but even back then I wouldn't tolerate that nonsense."

William, who was just getting out of the service, and Nellie Chase decided to move on. They thought about moving to Los Angeles but were frightened by the specter of earthquakes. Nellie had a friend who worked for the General Electric Company in Bridgeport. The decision was made. Shortly after their move Nellie became the first black registered nurse at St. Vincent's Hospital in Bridgeport. William Sr. worked as a machinist foreman at the Bridgeport Brass Company, one of the city's industrial powerhouses.

They both agreed that Billy was to be raised Roman Catholic. He attended all-white parochial schools and church at St. Augustine's Cathedral, where he sang in the church choir and was an altar boy.

Billy reports, "There weren't many black Catholics. My parents raised me to get along with everybody—not to hate all whites, which was an image they could have fostered after what they went through. We talked about race relations all the time. They would say that everyone is equal. They encouraged a positive outlook. 'Be proud of who you are and don't judge a person by their color. You should be judged by your ability, and when you're not then you should speak up.' They kept me optimistic."

Billy Chase played hoops in the basketball capital of Connecticut. He shot with the best competition in Bridgeport.

The Central High School gymnasium, where he played, smelled like a sweaty sock. The air was thick from the heated bodies of two thousand students—black, white, brown—shoe-horned into the bleachers; students right on top of the action, screaming wildly at their dripping-wet heroes, ten thoroughbred teenagers sprinting back and forth like race horses, their sweat and passion for the game mixing with the intensity from their rabid schoolmates in the stands.

It was the winter of 1976. Some of the purest high school basketball talent in the country was doing what they did best—showing off. Inner-city kids who had mastered their wide-open style in the playgrounds. Spin moves. Between-the-legs moves. Driving, twisting, turning, jamming-in-your-face moves.

"Hey, Billy, your house or your mama." *Swish.*

"Hey, John, check this." *Swish.*

Squeaky Converse sneakers. Furious action. Elbows flying in all directions. Heated rivalries feeding youthful egos. It was just a matter of time before a fight broke out.

Central's Antony Hopkins—"Hop," as everyone called him, street-wild, menacing-looking, sturdily-built, from one of Bridgeport's toughest housing projects—drives for a layup.

Whack.

Phil Murphy, Harding's jump-out-of-the-gym center, hacks him across the back. The referee's whistle blows. At this point, who cares about a whistle.

"Hey, motherfucker, what's your problem," Hopkins screams at Murphy.

"Fuck you."

"Fuck *you*," retorts Hopkins, shoving Murphy, who responds in kind. Harding's future NBA players John Bagley and Wes Mathews jump in.

"Okay, it's time to fight," Billy Chase yells at Harding, coming to his teammates' assistance.

A stray elbow here, a shove in the back there, and instantly the basketball court is a battlefield. Arms, legs, and fists zero in on anything within reach. The Zebras—the dark-striped, pot-bellied referees—look comical trying to pull apart the energized bodies of young men in the prime of condition, blowing their brains out on their whistles, hoping to restore sanity to a chaotic break in the action.

In the stands the noise is ear-splitting. School security is staked out at every gym entrance, keeping their watchful eyes on the students freaking out in the bleachers. As usual, it's too late. The court intensity infects the crowd. Someone throws a punch at a student from a rival team and mass hysteria erupts in the stands, bodies leap over bodies, sweaters are pulled over heads, hands grab mops of hair. The Central gym becomes a complete mad house.

Fortunately, no one pulls out a gun. People in the stands pull apart the crazy ones. Back on the court, the players decided they'd rather juke it out then duke it out. The game resumes. A broken nose in the stands, a bloody lip on the court—nothing too serious.

After all, this is Harding versus Central. The question isn't whether a fight will break loose, but how many fights and how serious they will be.

High school basketball rivalries in Bridgeport's inner city are high-jumpin', run-and-gun games of pure talent, producing NBA players Walter Luckett, John Garris, Wes Mathews, John Bagley, and Charles Smith. Bridgeport enjoys the finest talent in the state with the hottest rivalries.

"We had some intense basketball rivalries at Central. So intense we used to receive death threats. When we played at Harding we were escorted in by police. Fights in the stands, weapons all over

CHASED

the place. It was funny. The blacks and the Portuguese at Central never got along until basketball season, when Harding became the common foe. I'll never forget one day at school, all of a sudden this van pulls up and these Portuguese guys bolt out of it. It was like watching a movie. They empty out of the van with chains and bats and just whipped ass on the blacks. They all looked like Conan the Barbarian. It was like a battleground, all these guys on the ground all fucked up. We were saying, 'Damn, did you see that?' The cops came and broke it up. Back then it was chains and bats. Today it's guns.

"So after that the blacks had to get revenge. Dean Perkins, a nice guy who now works for the Connecticut State Police in the Narcotics Division, was one of the ring leaders. He was a big fucking guy. He had a gang. So he merged his gang with another gang. The plan was to beat up all the white people they saw. Any time a white person came down the hallway they beat him up. Instead of them just going after Portuguese, they were going after anything white.

"This wasn't the brightest strategy. What this did was turn everyone against the blacks. Then it got really chaotic. The cops had dogs up at Central; they had a police officer on every corner of the hallway. I used to shoot craps in the bathroom for a couple of dollars. One time I had the dice in my hands and I was shaking them while I was walking down the hallway. So the cop grabs my hand and takes my dice. I said, 'Damn, why are you taking my dice? I paid a dollar-fifty for those dice.' The cops were all over the place. It was like living in a prison."

☐ ☐ ☐

Billy Chase is not a fighter by nature, but if a fight broke out he was ready to throw down. If threatened by anyone, just in case things got too hot, he knew he could always count on Hop, the

Billy Chase & Lennie Grimaldi

enforcer. Billy met Hopkins through the city's summer basketball league, games pitting one housing project against another. If this crowd had had a bumper sticker, it would have read: "Give Blood, Play Ball in the Summer Basketball League." Billy played for Greene's Apartments, Hopkins for Beardsley Terrace. It was here they became acquainted, and it was here that they had their first confrontation.

It happened one June evening when the two teams clashed. As the action intensified, Hopkins caught an elbow in the face and thought Billy fired the shot.

"You really want to get your ass kicked today, don't you?" Hopkins yelled at Billy.

"It wasn't me," Billy said.

"Like hell it wasn't you."

"It wasn't me," Billy said definitively.

Hopkins charged at Billy. Billy stood his ground. They were pulled apart. "They'll be other days," Hopkins stalked away. Billy knew he meant it; Hopkins had a memory like IBM.

☐ ☐ ☐

Billy worked at the Beardsley Terrace housing project, which happened to be Hopkins's home turf, doing maintenance work for the city's federally funded Comprehensive Employment Training Act. Every day he was there Billy looked over his shoulder. Word was out that Hopkins wanted to get even for the elbow.

This was not good news. Hopkins was the kind of guy you did not want to get into a fight with. He was a man among boys, a cock-strong six-foot-three, two hundred pounds, owning a crazed look to match his size.

One afternoon Hopkins showed up.

"All my friends around me—everyone—left the area," Billy says. "Their attitude was 'See you later, you're on your own.' My

C H A S E D

brother, Nelson, was a big help, too. As he walked away he had this look on his face like, 'Man, after you get fucked up, I'll call the doctor to get you some medical attention.'"

These were the inner-city streets of Bridgeport. While a courtyard battle may lacerate the body in the short term, the long-term blow to the ego for backing down could cause one's reputation irreparable damage.

Hopkins stood menacingly right in front of Billy. Billy set his jaw. "I didn't elbow you, Hop, but if you want to fight, we'll fight." He waited for the first blow to be struck. Billy swallowed hard. He didn't want to fight, but even so, he would not back down to Hopkins. A long moment passed. Then Hopkins grinned. Billy had won Hopkins's respect. "No," Hopkins told him, "I was just coming down to say wass'up. What's done is done."

Billy had guts, but he preferred to use his brains. Hopkins owned a lot more guts than brains. Their personalities meshed. They developed a special bond that carried over as teammates on the Central High School basketball team, where they shared a common enemy—the Harding Presidents.

"If I got into a fight, Hop jumped in. If Hop got into a fight I'd jump in to help," Billy said.

Hopkins's battles went beyond basketball, though. He was considered the "baddest dude" in the school, and he didn't mind proving his reputation.

One day, Billy, Hopkins, and Bud Jackson, one of their classmates, were in the bathroom combing their hair and admiring their good looks in the mirror. Billy played instigator.

"Hop, you're supposed to be the baddest dude in Central. Who's this Jackson?"

"I'll tell you who I am, motherfucker," Jackson responded in Hopkins general direction. "You ain't shit."

"Oh, really," Hopkins said and grabbed him.

Within seconds, Hopkins and Jackson were rolling around on

the floor while Billy watched. They bounced off the walls, running into stalls, busting each other up. Blood spurted all over. The whole bathroom shook. Finally, Hopkins pinned Jackson down on the floor, which meant Jackson had had enough. Billy spent the day carrying the message to everyone in school that "Hop and Jackson rumbled in the bathroom and Hop's *still* the baddest dude in school."

After graduation, Billy, the honor student, and Hopkins, the enforcer, split apart, their lives going in opposite directions.

"Hop turned out to be one of the biggest heroin dealers in Bridgeport and later was sent up on a murder charge," Billy said. But Billy could not forget their bond.

"When I became a cop the feds asked me to do the case. That was the only case I refused to do. I told them I went to high school with this guy. I just couldn't do him. Back in those days when you got into a fight, you had to have guys on the team that would back you up. Everyone else would act like they didn't see anything. I could depend on Hop to back me up in a fight. I wanted to remember him like that."

☐   ☐   ☐

Billy graduated from Central with honors and was weighing an offer to attend and play basketball at Fairfield University, a respected Jesuit college. FU, as some called it, was a good school for Billy, close to home in neighboring Fairfield, and academically prestigious. Joe Carter, who built a respectable Division I basketball program at Fairfield University, put on a coach's schmooze in his college office.

"We have a great program here," Carter told Billy, who was looking over the contract for a scholarship. "We'll be playing a few games at Madison Square Garden against top competition. You'll like it here."

CHASED

Billy had pen in hand, ready to sign the contract. Before he signed, Carter had one more thing to add.

"I'll be frank with you, Billy. Every nigger I get in here fucks up."

Billy listened in stunned silence. If this was a way for a coach to keep his "nigger" down, Billy wasn't buying it. "I'll get back to you," Billy told Carter and walked out of his office. Billy said later, "I told FU to FU."

Neighboring Sacred Heart University, the liberal arts commuter college founded by the Roman Catholic Diocese of Bridgeport, made Billy an offer he couldn't refuse.

"Sacred Heart was giving up some money. I got a car when I signed to go there, a full-boat scholarship, and they paid for my living expenses. They put me up in an apartment, and then we had an account that we could use at any time to get money. My mother called the coach one day inquiring about this car I received. She was practically ready to turn me over to the NCAA."

One of Sacred Heart's star basketball players, Willie Boyd, told Billy just how to play it.

"The coach is going to call you in and offer to put you on a partial scholarship," Boyd told Billy. "All you have to do is say, 'Forget it, I'll go someplace else on a full scholarship.' And the minute you get up to go out the door, he's going to call you back and offer you a full scholarship."

Billy met with Coach Don Feeley, and just as Boyd explained, the coach said, "The best I can do is give you a partial scholarship."

Billy got out of his seat and walked to the door: "Forget about it, I'll go someplace else."

"Wait, wait," Feeley said to Billy. "Let's talk about it."

Beyond the door, Billy could hear Boyd waiting out in the hallway laughing his ass off. The coach offered Billy a full scholarship including books, tuition, and living expenses.

"I said, this is cool," Billy said. "They gave me a check to buy a car. I bought a Toyota Corolla, a four-speed. Every time I needed money I went to the coach. He gave me a voucher and I'd take the voucher to the office and they'd cut me a check and I'd go to the bank and cash it.

"Dudes had great stereos, cars, cash. SHU paid our rent, paid for our standard phone bill, paid for all of our furniture, and kept our refrigerator full of meat from the American Frozen Food Company.

"What a life. We always had money. All because we could put a ball into a basket. One time the coach gave me $40 to take a prospective recruit out to eat. I took the kid to McDonald's and pocketed the rest."

☐   ☐   ☐

Coach Feeley left Sacred Heart under a cloud of controversy. A new coach was brought in—David Bike, who would lead his team to a Division II national championship in 1987.

"Things were supposed to get even better," Billy said. "Bike comes in and changes everything, restructures the whole program. One pair of sneakers for the season. No extras. I know he was doing the right thing, but we were spoiled. He was so goddamn cheap. He gave me a dollar once; I swear he took the dollar out and I watched him put sunglasses on it. It hadn't seen light in years. But then the alumni came through. They took care of us. They had their own club, big corporate types, executives from Olin, and after the game, the players would socialize with the alumni.

"We had a few drinks together in the Pioneer Room. Bike wouldn't let them give us money, so we'd give them a ticket and they'd give $75 for the ticket. I had a twin-size bed. I told them I was having back problems and couldn't sleep comfortably. They said, 'What do you need?' I told them, 'I need a queen-size bed.' I had it in two days. Another time the clutch went on my car. The

CHASED

alumni guys replaced it for me. Finally, Bike holds a big meeting and says you can't give these guys money, it's against NCAA rules. We got away with murder.

"We were like big stars. Women were all over us. We were running through them. We used to make bets. We'd be sitting in the cafeteria eyeing the women, and we'd say, 'Okay, I'll bet you a six pack of Heineken that I'll get her over the house tonight.' Then the dudes would be over the house, staked out, so they could see her. She'd be in the room and when she came out the beer was on the table. She'd leave and then we would celebrate. We were so bad, one girl gave us all Bibles to read. I guess she wanted us to cleanse our souls. Willie Boyd apparently took it to heart. He's now a preacher at a Bridgeport church."

With all the attention and adulation, Billy didn't complete his studies. He left SHU six credits shy of his degree. But who needed a degree with visions of playing professional basketball in Europe for the Dutch national team?

They offered Billy $35,000 to start, a car, and free lodging. But Billy had damaged his knee in his junior year. During a game against the University of Loyola, he had jumped for a rebound and came down on a player's foot, turning and tearing his knee and thigh muscle. When the recruiter came over to see Billy, Billy was on crutches.

"That was it," Billy said. "My basketball career was all done."

CHAPTER 3

Corrections

AFTER BILLY LEFT Sacred Heart and realized that his basketball days were behind him, he examined his career choices. Law enforcement was a profession that had always interested him. In 1980, with the intention of using the experience as a stepping stone into police work, he applied for a position with the Connecticut Department of Corrections, took the test for a corrections officer, and scored an 89.

Billy says, "I went through an interview process and heard nothing further other than that I was a good candidate. Beyond that no one could tell me if I would be hired."

At the urging of his mother, Billy went to see State Senator Margaret Morton, a grandmotherly funeral home operator whose husband had gone to embalming school in New York with Billy's father. A soft-spoken, dignified woman, Senator Morton, the granddaughter of slaves, had successfully challenged the political machine of charismatic Bridgeport Mayor John Mandanici with charges of corruption and ethnic tensions.

The city had failed to get to the bottom of an arson problem tormenting inner-city neighborhoods, principally the residential areas of blacks and Puerto Ricans. Residents living in ramshackle tenements and in the horrors of ceaseless fires were convinced that "Mandy" and the cops were not investigating the suspicious fires because white landlords were benefiting from insurance claims.

The evidence was strong that nobody gave a damn. Even when people were killed in the fires, the investigations were merely for show. At that, the city's police and fire departments fought over whose responsibility it was and who should be in charge.

Fire officials maintained that since the fires were arsons, fire officers should lead investigation teams. Police officials maintained that since the arsons were crimes, they should lead investigation teams. The mayor, uncharacteristically quiet on the matter, let the cops and firefighters slug it out with each other in the newspapers and did little to break the logjam, claiming it was up to the Civil Service Commission to decide.

The citizens on the Civil Service Commission didn't seem too interested, either, nor did the citizens on the Police Commission or the Fire Commission. After all, they were all appointed by Mandanici.

Meanwhile, Bridgeport burned. Some black and Puerto Rican kids started torching the empty shells of half-burnt buildings.

A couple of inner-city residents thought they would beat the landlords at their own game and get better welfare-financed housing if they were burned out of their East Side tenement. Unfortunately, the arsonist showed up when everybody was home. Seven people burned to death, and more than a dozen innocents were injured by the scheme, which horrified all Bridgeporters—black, white, and brown.

That atrocity was solved; most went unpunished.

CHASED

Minority groups in increasing numbers believed their mayor didn't care about them. To stem fury and alienation, Mandy allowed Puerto Rican community leaders to pick a young lawyer, a native of the city's housing projects, who had successfully completed college and law school and was hanging up a legal shingle in town, to serve on the police board. After nearly two years of frustration in getting the cops or the mayor to listen to his people, the enraged young lawyer Eddie Rodriguez changed his party affiliation to Republican, declaring: "I'm not going to be anybody's house Spic."

There was more. One winter's day turned into sorrow and horror with the squeeze of a trigger. At one moment, Police Officer Gerald DiJoseph drove his cruiser into the underground garage of an apartment building. Why? Was he trying to stop a motor vehicle for a violation? No one knows. DiJoseph didn't radio in.

In the next moment, he was shot dead, the first officer killed in the line of duty in more than fifty years.

The police response was instantaneous. Acting on a rumor that a black man was seen in the vicinity, Police Superintendent Joseph A. Walsh ordered every black social club, every black bottle club, and every bar in Bridgeport frequented by blacks closed.

Police were convinced that by rousting the community they would get the tips needed to track down the cop killer. It never happened. Police were more successful in achieving another, unintended reaction. The black community was roused against the Police Department and Mayor Mandanici, organizing protest meetings, political action committees, and vowing revenge.

They didn't have long to wait to get it, politically at least.

Bridgeport State Senator Salvatore DePiano had decided to hang up his senate career, keeping only his city position as tax attorney with cozy city health benefits.

The decision set off a mad scramble of potential successors. Heading the list was Margaret Morton, an eight-year veteran of the

State House of Representatives and senior member of the Bridgeport delegation who fought against the most seasoned and cold-blooded politicians in the city. She didn't fit the Bridgeport profile of a candidate: she wasn't male, and she wasn't white. The ballot said DePiano versus Morton, but in reality it was an us-against-them, black-versus-white, good-versus-evil machine street war.

When it was over, Morton had won by eight votes. Her victory invigorated a black community that had garnered little attention from party leaders, and led to Mandanici's election defeat by a Republican challenger the following year. Even the black community voted for the Republican—and the Puerto Ricans were right with them.

To many white people in Connecticut, Morton, the first black woman state senator in Connecticut, was a symbol of sanity in a city gone mad. True, she was black in an overwhelmingly white state, but she was openly emotional, loving, and caring, her word was good, and she was honest.

Billy says, "I explained the situation to Margaret. The only thing I knew was that I scored well on the test and they had told me that I was a good candidate, but beyond that I hadn't heard a thing. Margaret said she would make a call for me.

"The next day someone in Corrections called me. They said, Where have you been? We've been looking for you. We have a job for you. I told them I've been here all the time. They hired me as a corrections guard. They assigned me to the Whaley Avenue Corrections facility."

The Whaley Avenue Correctional Center in New Haven was a prison guard's nightmare. It housed the state's most helpless and hopeless criminals—murderers, stick-up men, leg breakers, scam artists, rapists. The jail offered an interesting contrast to the hefty ivy walls and aristocracy of Yale University just minutes away.

Inside the guts of the jail, corrections officers were responsible for eight counts a day. They did everything from supervising

CHASED

prisoner work details to accounting for all the disposable plastic Bic razors they handed out for the inmates to shave with. Lockdown was 11:00 P.M. In summer the five-by-ten-foot cells with metal mesh screens simmered like ovens. Some of the cells housed two prisoners.

"If you had a cellmate and homeboy had the runs, you were all through," Billy said.

The confines tested the patience of criminal and corrections officer alike.

The corrections officers who were assigned to keep the peace in the state-run facility survived on their wits. They could not carry weapons. They'd check their gun when they arrived at work and pick it up when they left for home. No gun, no night stick, no blackjack, no Mace. This was to keep weapons away from a dangerous prison population. If a riot broke out, prison officials called in the State Police. The explosive environment forced the guards to develop special skills to move men who were already serving life terms and had nothing left to lose. In such an atmosphere a reputation was critical. If the inmates smelled a wimp, they'd walk all over the guard . . . or worse.

In his first year, Billy watched seventy corrections officers come and go, victims of the pressures of dealing with dangerous and defiant criminals. COs got by on reputation and mental toughness. Their life expectancy was just a couple of months.

Billy wondered how long he'd last. He received an early education. One evening he was preparing to leave his work station to go to the officers mess hall. As required before leaving, he had to account for all the prisoners in his cell block heading into the dining room. Billy kept a watch on the inmates moving along. Then, he was distracted by prisoner Troy Green, six-foot-six, 220 pounds, pounding on a glass partition separating him from Billy's work station.

"CO, I want to talk to you. Let me out of my cell."

"Not now, I'm busy. We'll talk later."

The banging persisted.

"What's your problem?" Billy shot back.

"The next time I want to leave my cell you better let me out."

"You don't run this block, I do."

"Let's find out who runs this block."

"You're not talking to me, are you?"

"I'm talking to you."

Billy exploded. "I'm gonna bust that ass." Billy opened the door to Green's cell area and rushed after him. Other COs tried to restrain Billy.

"Let me go. I want that ass," Billy said.

"C'mon," Green said.

The riot squad was called in to break them up. They surrounded Billy, yanked him away, and ordered him to cool off. Billy's supervisor, John Salvas, lectured Billy with some sobering words of advice.

"If you're going to pick on somebody, why do you have to pick on somebody who's doing a basketball score for a sentence?" Salvas told Billy. "This guy's doing ninety-nine years for murder. He has nothing to lose."

Billy got the message. "Okay, you're right. I'm cool, I'm calm."

Billy learned quickly that among killers, a CO's reputation was just about everything. And it seemed as though Billy had more violent criminals per square inch assigned to his block then any other CO. Keith Laws was one of them. They had transferred him from the Bridgeport Correctional Center jail, where he punched out a lieutenant and two guards. Laws was built like Arnold Schwarzeneggar, six-foot-four, 250 pounds, and he could disconnect a man with his bare hands. Nobody fucked with him. In fact, Billy was told, don't even go near him.

One night, Laws was in a restless mood and wanted his new

CHASED

cell cleaned out and his mattress fumigated.

"CO, let me out, I want my cell cleaned."

"Can't this wait until tomorrow?" Billy responded.

"No, I want to clean it out *now*," Laws reiterated, banging on the cell.

There was a familiar ring to Laws's voice, one that brought Billy back years. He flashed a light in Laws's face. Upon inspection, a smile broadened Billy's face.

"Keith Laws, is that you?"

"Oh, shit, Chase, man, what are you doing here?"

"I'm your worst nightmare," Billy added with a wink, "and I'm definitely not here to switch places with you."

Laws was the younger brother of an old pal in Bridgeport. Laws had looked up to Billy. When they were kids, Billy had once wrestled Laws to the ground and ordered him to pick up some goodies at the store when he was hungry. Through the years they lost contact. Since then, Keith Laws had grown up, and no one was too interested in ordering him around anymore. Fortunately, no one in the cell block was aware of Billy's relationship with Laws.

"Hey Keith," Billy whispered, "do me a favor." Laws was a willing partner in Billy's conspiracy. Billy returned to his station and flicked on the sound system.

"Hey, Laws, hurry and finish up your cell, we don't have all night!" Billy shouted over the cell block loud speaker for everyone to hear.

"Fuck you," Laws responded. "I'll finish when I'm ready. You don't like it go stick your head up your ass."

Billy bolted into Laws's cell, grabbed the big man, and pushed him up against the wall.

"Listen, I'll kick your ass! When I tell you to do something, you better do it!"

"Okay, okay, Chase, no problem," Laws replied meekly, winking at Billy.

29

Word got around the prison real fast. "Don't fuck with Chase," the inmates would say.

"My attitude about corrections work was to be fair, but don't take any shit. I treated the prisoners like human beings first. But if you act like an animal, I'm going to treat you like an animal. I felt I could fall asleep in my block. I could leave my door open with inmates walking by, I had that much control over them. It was like listening to a symphony, nobody fighting or arguing, guys playing dominoes and checkers.

"But then you always had to be prepared for the day they say, 'We need you upstairs.' It was like going to the Bronx Zoo—motherfuckers hanging from the ceiling and going crazy. A friend of mine who went to Sacred Heart with me—he was a nice, easygoing guy—he got ulcers from working in the jail. The stress of dealing with crazy people. No gun. No club. No Mace. No protection. When you're in the general population, you're in there with nothing but yourself."

Tempers were short, especially when an inmate was accused of abusing his phone time. One evening a CO, Jed Carter, ordered Hank Roberts, a prisoner who was chatting with his girlfriend, off the phone.

Carter called out, "Off the phone, Roberts. Your time is up."

Roberts reddened. "What's your problem? Just give me another minute."

Carter demanded, "Your time is done."

Roberts went nuts. He grabbed a homemade weapon, a shiv, the metal piece on the end of a mop he had sharpened, jumped the guard, held him down, and was about to split his head open.

As Roberts was coming down with the metal piece, Billy pounced on him, pinning the inmate down.

"He would have killed the officer," Billy said. "All because the guy had to get off the phone. Some people in there didn't give a fuck about themselves and cared less about you."

C H A S E D

As much as the heterosexual population was a cause for consternation, even more troubling were "the rump rangers," as the straight inmates called them.

"Sometimes when they opened their door it was like someone put Spanish Fly in their drink—the whole floor was like one big orgy," Billy says. "It was like chaos; guys would be running into the cell for sex. They'd go right at it, like dogs in heat. We had to break them up. Any kind of sex they could do, they would be doing it."

One night as Billy approached the cell, three of them jumped him. They unleashed a series of elbows, kicks, punches, and scratches. Someone failed to tell them that Billy was training for his black belt in karate.

He grabbed one inmate and threw him in his cell, punched two others silly, and threw them into their cells. Exhausted, Billy leaned up against a cell for relief.

"Damn," he said, "this is crazy."

Herb Arons, another inmate who watched the action, was peeking through his cell.

"Hey, Chase?"

"Hey, what," Billy responded.

"They almost got your ass, didn't they?"

"Fuck you," Billy said and walked away.

Billy says, "If I had become a police officer before I experienced corrections, I might have been a screwed-up cop. Corrections helped me develop special skills in dealing with people under difficult conditions. That's where I learned my education about scams that are run. If you can survive working in a prison and you go into police work, you'll make one hell of a cop. Every cop I know who was a corrections officer was a great cop. A lot of cops feel that if they put that badge on they're God. They can do anything they want to anyone they want. You see, when you're dealing with people in a jail setting, you have no guns, no night stick, no blackjack. It forces you to use your head in dealing with bad situations."

CHAPTER 4

The Connecticut Crew

On September 19, 1981, at approximately 2:45 p.m., Billy Chase was walking north on Main Street in Bridgeport for a Saturday afternoon pick-up basketball game at Sheridan School.

The popping sound of gunfire several blocks ahead roused his curiosity. When Billy arrived at the corner of Main and Jewett he saw police personnel, an ambulance, and a large crowd of onlookers. He walked closer. There lay the bullet-riddled body of Frank "Cigars" Piccolo, the most powerful mobster in Connecticut. The gunblasts that Billy had heard forever changed organized crime's rule in Connecticut. They would also have a profound impact on Billy and what he later perceived as the mission of his life.

□   □   □

Piccolo was a captain in the Carlo Gambino organized crime family, which controlled a major portion of illegal loansharking, gambling, and drug activities in the state. He had just finished making a telephone call from a public phone booth at one of the busiest intersections in the city, a few blocks north of Billy's house.

As Piccolo hung up the phone, a maroon van pulled alongside the curb. Two masked men with rifles jumped out. "Hey, Frank, this is for you," one of the gunmen said. They blasted him with two .30-caliber semi-automatic rifles. One of the bullets blew apart his wrist, another drilled a one-inch hole in his chest, a perfect bullseye through George Washington's demure face in the roll of dollar bills stored in the gangster's shirt pocket. Piccolo lay sprawled in a pool of blood as the van took off. Within a half-hour, the most powerful mobster in Connecticut was dead.

A short time later, a Trumbull, Connecticut, police officer monitoring the Bridgeport Police radio spotted the getaway van and made a high-speed chase through suburban Trumbull and north Stratford. Escaping through a fence opening, the van entered the backyard of the home of Gus Curcio, a soldier in the rival Genovese crime family. The Trumbull officer, warned by his superiors on the radio of a possible ambush, didn't pursue further.

Witnesses described the driver of the van as a man in his early thirties with light brown hair and a beard. The description fit Gus Curcio, and a warrant for his arrest was issued. Three days later, a clean-shaven Gus Curcio walked into Bridgeport police headquarters maintaining he was framed. He was charged with conspiracy to commit murder but was never tried. A state grand jury, whose proceedings were closed to the public, refused to indict Curcio.

It wasn't until many years later that a mob insider publicly fingered Paul Castellano, Godfather of the Gambino crime family, for ordering the Piccolo hit. Salvatore "Sammy the Bull" Gravano,

CHASED

John Gotti's underboss and close friend, became the government's star witness during Gotti's racketeering trial. In his testimony against his former boss, Gravano revealed that Castellano was "selling out the family for his own basic businesses. He had a captain who was in our family, Piccolo, killed and he used another family to do it." Gravano explained that this was one of several reasons for Gotti whacking Castellano.

"You just don't let another family kill a captain within your own family," Gravano testified. "That's against our rules, and nobody was happy with that."

Piccolo's murder capped a wacky and bloody list of mob-related hits in southwestern Connecticut.

One summer day in 1979, Salvatore "Midge Renault" Annunziato, of East Haven, a member of the Genovese crime family, left his house after receiving a phone call. He jumped into a car with Thomas "Tommy the Blond" Vastano, also a Genovese member. Annunziato was never seen, alive or dead, again.

Annunziato had been named by federal officials as a target in organized crime activities, for alleged racketeering, in the Bridgeport area. Police informants believed that Annunziato had been shot several times, secured to an anchor, and dumped into Bridgeport Harbor.

Annunziato's disappearance came three weeks before Carmine Galante, the most powerful mobster in New York, was gunned down in a Brooklyn restaurant while he sat with a cigar between his teeth.

Six months later, in January 1980, Vastano himself was found shot to death in the yard of his Stratford home. Vastano had been called to testify before a federal grand jury probing organized crime activities. "Oh no! Oh no!" were the last words heard by Vastano's neighbors before gunfire silenced him.

On April 2, 1980, Ralph "Whitey" Tropiano, another target of police for his Connecticut organized crime activities, was walking with his nephew along a Brooklyn, New York, street. Shots were fired from a passing car, hitting Tropiano in the head and chest.

Five days later, William Shamansky was hit by a bullet during a wild shootout on the Merritt Parkway in the Bridgeport area. Shamansky reportedly had been squabbling over gambling and drug-related activities with Joseph Rabbit, a Piccolo enforcer. With guns blasting from both vehicles along several miles of the parkway and through residential streets, Shamansky was hit by a bullet and killed. Three days later, Rabbit was found slumped across the seat of his car in the parking lot of the Howard Johnson's in Stamford, a major mob hangout. He had been shot execution-style in the back of the head. The Ho-Jo's was coined by Stamford Advocate reporter Frank Fedeli the "Joe Rabbit Memorial Hotel."

Three months later, David "The Turk" Avnayim was found shot to death and dumped in a wooded section of rural Redding, Connecticut. Avnayim had been a target of organized crime investigations, suspected of drug dealing and arson.

A month before the Piccolo murder, John Gulbenkian, a key figure in state and federal organized crime investigations and an underworld drug supplier, and his young assistant Joseph Ourfalian were blasted to death by two gunmen in Gulbenkian's jewelry store in Bridgeport. Before he died, Ourfalian managed to get off two shots, killing one of the hitmen, Hell's Angels member Robert Erf. Although most Mafia members preferred to have work fulfilled within their own organized crime families, it was not uncommon for the mob to hire motorcycle club members as their enforcers.

Speculation ran rampant on the Piccolo rub out. U.S. Attorney Richard Blumenthal, whose forces had nailed Piccolo on two racketeering indictments just months before the shooting, said Piccolo was eliminated because the indictments brought publicity and embarrassment to the crime family.

Some of this embarrassment had been recorded about a year earlier. Between bites of his lunch at his Bridgeport Backstage

CHASED

Delicatessen Restaurant, Piccolo was lecturing his chief enforcer, Fred Cavuoto, on how important it was for organized crime to be covered by a blanket of legitimate business in case things got hot. Little did Piccolo know that, as he spoke, things for him were already red hot.

"Our people would be in all rackets and not legitimate if they thought like you," Piccolo told Cavuoto. "You understand? Why do you think they got so many legitimate businesses? Because tomorrow the rackets go down."

Cavuoto listened without interruption as his capo continued the history lesson. "Castro Convertible. Fifty years before when they started they were helped by people in Brooklyn. They stopped the people, and they helped them with a little money. They bought 'em off, they got the union, they got a piece. Ford . . . Ford . . ."

"Motor Company?" Cavuoto asked.

". . . Motor Company was helped by the Italians, greaseballs in Detroit and Chicago. Why do you think there was so many Italians that had agencies in the Ford?"

"Yeah, yeah," Cavuoto said.

"The thing, the thing in Jersey. Every car that came outta there was . . . in our family. There was a couple of guys that every car that came out they had the trailer trucks that delivered 'em. Everybody got something. Tell me you understand."

"Yeah, I do understand," Cavuoto responded.

Federal agents monitoring the conversation also understood. Thanks to Piccolo, Cavuoto got a first-hand education that day. And thanks to a bugging device that was secretly planted nearby, the FBI got a first-hand education about Piccolo and his crew.

At fifty-eight, Piccolo seemed to be sitting pretty. His closets were filled with five-hundred-dollar suits, his penthouse outfitted with lavish furniture. Reporting to Paul Castellano, the Gambino family boss in New York, Piccolo controlled most of the illegal crime activities in Connecticut: all the gambling, loansharking, and drug activities in southwestern Connecticut involving middle-class Bridgeport shop owners, affluent Stamford restaurateurs, and the down and out. Piccolo had little trouble with the law, on either local or federal levels. A few arrests on gambling charges, a few motor vehicle violations, an assault—all petty nonsense to a man who could, by the wave of a hand, order a man to be rubbed out. To those who didn't fear him, Piccolo was a warm, friendly guy—easy going, approachable. He rarely shouted or cursed. Piccolo commanded respect, lots of it. He was shrewd, ruthless, smart, canny, and opportunitistic.

But then, like a lot of men who believe they are unreachable, he slipped up. A two-month-long surveillance produced the evidence the feds believed they needed. Nearly seven hundred taped conversations between Piccolo and his acquaintances made from phones in his restaurant, his penthouse apartment, and Tony's Italian Restaurant in Stamford, Connecticut, led to charges of conspiracy to obstruct justice, conspiracy to commit murder, and, just in case that wasn't enough, violations of gambling, narcotics, and loansharking laws.

But it was a bigger case, one that plunged him into the national spotlight, that may have ultimately led to his undoing. Three months before his death, Piccolo was indicted in connection with a plot to extort money from singers Wayne Newton and Lola Falana. One of Piccolo's tapped phone conversations involved a discussion of the receipt of a hidden interest in the Aladdin Hotel which Newton co-owned. Falana was under contract to the Aladdin. It may have been Piccolo's carelessness in discussing syndicate secrets over the telephone that resulted in his death.

☐   ☐   ☐

The bloody sight of Piccolo's bullet-ridden body, the knowledge of what had been, and of the madness Piccolo and his friends

CHASED

had wreaked on Billy's community, and especially the young, was something Billy Chase never forgot. Although in the years to follow he was to capture many well-known drug lords in his career as an undercover cop, he kept his eye on his ultimate goal—the Mafia.

CHAPTER 5

Ebony and Ivory

WHILE EMPLOYED BY the State Corrections Department, Billy took the entry-level tests for both the Monroe and Bridgeport Police Departments, two towns that offered recruiting examinations. Riding a test score of 98, Billy received an offer from Monroe first, so Billy grabbed it, hopeful that an offer from his home town would come later.

Monroe, Connecticut, population 18,000, is a suburban community roughly ten miles north of Bridgeport that is home to young professionals and thousands of white former city residents who fled Bridgeport for the comforts of suburban life, better schools, spacious property, lower taxes, and less crime.

It's a picturesque town of white picket fences, carved stone walls, and old country homes featuring Georgian, Federal, Greek

Revival, and Victorian architecture. New housing developments and retail expansion have turned the community from a sleepy New England village into a rapidly developing suburb with modern conveniences.

Although most of Monroe's residents are second- and third-generation children of European immigrants who originally settled in Bridgeport, the town has a distinctive Old Yankee tradition. But beneath the Beaver Cleaver outward image lies a rattling skeleton, an intrigue for the supernatural for the tales residents tell about sorcery, witchcraft, and hocus-pocus. Vivid imaginations or not, at the top of every resident's list is the legendary town witch, Hannah Cranna, a wry mid–Nineteenth Century woman who would sit on her favorite rock and hurl curses at townspeople who dared cross her path. Lonely Hannah, so the legend goes, placed a curse on the town while on her death bed.

To this day, on moonlight evenings, travelers swear they've heard blood-curdling screams from the vicinity of the cemetery plot that is her resting place.

If Hannah Cranna makes townspeople nervous, the legendary Melon Heads terrify even the most cynical disbelievers. Monroe's Melon Heads are mysterious cantalouped-shaped mongoloids that kids swear they've encountered on the dark side of the town's voluminous woods and whose parents hope they never meet. The Melon Heads never really do anything terrible, they just scare the skivvies off of you, or so the kids say.

"If you move to Monroe, watch out for the Melon Heads," is the typical rejoinder to a new townie. "We've never seen any ourselves, but they're supposed to have this cross-eyed, inbred kind of look with huge, round, white heads. They live in the woods and only come out at night."

Complementing the town's mythical stories and ghostchasers, there have been some truly bizarre home-grown crimes in recent years.

CHASED

In one incident, a town resident who had been arguing with his wife picked up a sledgehammer and caved in her head. He then performed an instant burial. Days passed and the cops were scratching their heads for leads to the whereabouts of the bereaved man's missing wife. Then the cops chanced upon a tantalizing piece of information. The neighbor next door couldn't quite figure out why the man was pouring concrete for a brand new porch in his back yard at four in the morning. He told this to the police, who promptly ripped up the concrete patio, drove shovels into the ground, and discovered the woman's body. The story of the man who hammered his wife to death and then buried her in the back yard receives as much gossipy attention in town as the Melon Heads.

☐ ☐ ☐

In this bedroom community known for its suburban charm, unique supernatural tales, and bizarre crime stories, Billy Chase too became a whispered-about topic in January 1983. The first black police officer in the town's history, he joined a department with twenty-five cops and three patrol cars on duty. The starting pay was three hundred dollars per week.

"When I wanted to hire Billy, one commissioner was opposed to having a black officer," says Monroe Police Chief Robert Wesche, adding that Monroe only had one opening at the time. "I had suspected that might be an issue with some people. But the commission voted unanimously to hire him. Billy did not come on because he was black. He was hired because he was the most qualified. I was impressed with his intelligence and interest in people."

Monroe had—and still does have—only a handful of blacks living in town, so when blacks are seen the general reaction among townies is that they must be from Bridgeport or another big city. As a result, some of the folks who live there aren't the most racially sensitive people in the world. Billy hadn't given much thought to this until one afternoon while on patrol, when he picked up a sandwich at the town diner, a popular hangout for locals and police alike. Within minutes of getting back in his patrol car, Billy received a call on the car radio.

"We have a report of a black guy impersonating a police officer at the diner."

"You're kidding," Billy replied. "I was just there and didn't notice a thing."

"You should check it out."

Billy turned around and returned to the diner.

"Excuse me," he asked the patrons and workers at the eatery, "I understand someone here called in a complaint about a black guy impersonating a cop. Anybody know about this?"

"Yeah," said one of the patrons, a balloon-faced fiftyish man. "I called it in."

"Do you remember what he looked like and when he left?"

"Yes, Officer, he looked just like you and left a few minutes ago."

"He looked just like me?"

"Yes, Officer."

"How much like me?"

The man did a doubletake and his face deflated. "Just like you, Officer," he said sheepishly.

"I just picked up lunch here a few minutes ago. Do you suppose I was the one you called about?"

"Yeah, Officer, I guess so."

Just days on the job in the rather odd town of Monroe, and Billy's first investigation was "my damn self!"

☐   ☐   ☐

For a man raised in the inner city, Billy found life as a suburban cop to be a cultural shocker. Monroe was as much rural in its

C   H   A   S   E   D

appearance and mindset as it was suburban. If featured its share of farmers who lived off the land and provided milk to townies. One morning, Billy received another call from dispatch.

"We have a report of a missing cow over on Hattertown Road."

"That's just great," Billy said to himself. "What the fuck am I going to do about a missing cow?"

To his own surprise, Billy had learned how to retrieve a stray cow in the state police academy but never thought he'd actually have to bring one back to its owner. He visited the farmer.

"Sir, what's the trouble?"

"My cow left my property and I can't find it."

"Well, which way do you suppose it went?"

"Thataway, over there," said the farmer, pointing toward a field.

Billy surveyed the area. It didn't take long for him to spot the cow. "Damn," he said. "How am I going to get this thing home? I can't drag his ass back."

Billy followed the procedure he learned at the academy: He peeled a hub cap off of his police cruiser, dropped some pebbles in the middle, and walked toward the bovine. Billy shook the hub cap as if it were a pot producing popcorn over a stove. The idea is to entice the cow to think there's food in the hubcap.

"C'mon cow, c'mon cow," Billy urged her on. "Just think of me as the Pied Piper. Come and get the goodies in my hand."

Hook, line, sinker—here comes Billy and the cow right behind him across the field, down the street, and back to the waiting arms of her thankful owner.

"I really put my life on the line that time," Billy says laughing.

Worse yet was the day he played dog catcher. The dog warden was out sick and Billy received a call about a roaming dog. He hopped into the canine truck, drove to the house, and pulled out the dog retriever—a long stick with a rope attached at the end which is designed to grab the dog by the neck and haul it into the truck. This might have been a routine assignment, but Billy was deathly afraid of dogs. He hoped he wouldn't see this one. To his dismay, he soon spotted the animal.

"Damn," Billy complained. "What am I going to do about this dog?" The brown-haired mutt looked placid and approachable, so Billy moved slowly forward and reached out his hand as a sign of friendship. "Nice dog, good dog. I'm your friend, it's okay." The dog recoiled, his snout sneered, his eyes darkened. When the dog snarled, baring teeth and coming at him, there was only one thing to do. Billy dropped the stick and ran.

At record speed he jumped into the truck. He was quite aware that every day he was a corrections officer, the possibility existed that some killer could rip his throat out. But there's nothing quite like the reality of a snarling, toothy animal jumping at your neck. Billy sighed sitting there in the truck. He noticed a group of kids who decided to play audience to this embarrassing encounter. It was time to pull together some courage.

The kids hunkered down in the grass for a close-up look at a not so friendly confrontation with man's best friend.

"C'mon, Mr. Police Officer, don't be afraid," the kids mocked. "He won't hurt you."

Billy wasn't encouraged. He climbed out of the truck and picked up the retriever. He approached the dog carefully, trying to get close enough to apply the noose around the dog's neck. This was not at all acceptable to the animal. All of a sudden the dog bolted. Billy chased after it, running in circles around the house——slipping, sliding, and falling in the dirt along the way. Every time he took a turn around the house he could hear the pesky little kids laughing.

"He went that way." "No, he went that way." "No, the dog's over there."

Finally, feeling humiliated, Billy dove at the dog's legs and tripped up the pooch, grabbed it, and tossed the rope around his

CHASED

neck. He tossed the dog into the canine truck, planning to take it to the pound.

"Hey, Mr. Police Officer, do it again," the kids yelled.

The kids had a good laugh, but Billy felt like a wreck.

Unfortunately, it was a feeling that came back again. It would not have been a day on the job in Monroe if Billy hadn't received a call about a smashed mailbox. Baseball-bat wielding kids loved to use them for target practice, especially during the Halloween season. On All Hallows Eve, Billy got a dispatch. "We have a call for a vandalized mailbox on Lover's Lane." Billy responded.

"Hello, sir, I heard you had some trouble with a mailbox."

"Yeah, Officer, the kids came through with a baseball bat."

"Did you see or hear anything?"

"Well, no, not really."

"How much is your mailbox worth?"

"Well, I don't know if I can put a price on it."

"Why not?"

"Because I stole it."

When he finished that call another dispatch came in: "We have a report of a driver who ran his car into the woods off Jockey Hollow Road." Once again Billy responded, this time to find a sleepy doctor behind the wheel of his car. The gray-haired, friendly-faced doctor was an accommodating fellow, and Billy saw no reason to give him a harder time than he had already experienced.

"So what happened, sir?"

"Oh, I ran my car off the road."

"I can see that. What was the reason?"

"I was a little tired."

"But just a minute ago you told me that an animal ran in front of your car and you ran off the road to avoid hitting it."

"Officer, that's exactly what happened. There was a cat or something and I tried not to hit the poor thing and ran off the road."

Billy let the guy drive off. He only damaged his car and had suffered enough aggravation.

It wasn't the last time Billy ran into the doctor. About a year later Billy went for his psychological examination, which is standard policy for entry into the Bridgeport Police Department. He walked into the office of the examiner, who was sitting in his chair, his back facing the door. The doctor wheeled around, faced Billy, and smiled. "I don't know why they sent you here for a psychological. You're already a cop in Monroe. And I think that you're a damn good cop. I ought to know."

"Thanks, doc," Billy said.

☐ ☐ ☐

In the months to follow, Billy developed a special place in his heart for bringing home stray cows, chasing runaway dogs, writing up mailbox vandalism, and sending home sleepy doctors. In fact, such quaint adventures were commonplace—at least when compared to his bizarre encounter with ghostchasers Ed and Lorraine Warren. The Warrens are considered among the country's leading authorities on the subject of spirits and supernatural phenomena. The Monroe residents have travelled the world investigating thousands of paranormal and ghostly disturbances, including the infamous Amityville Horror case.

One chilly autumn day, Billy was dispatched to the Warrens' house after the ghostbusters received a weird death threat. From the street someone had fired a hunting arrow through the Warrens' picture window. The arrow had a note attached: "You won't be among the living much longer."

Billy hesitated as he rang the doorbell. He didn't believe in ghosts, but he didn't really want to go into the house everyone referred to as haunted.

Ed Warren invited Billy through the front door. Billy looked around creepily. He noticed a dog at the top of the steps leading to the second floor. The dog wouldn't come down the stairs.

"What's wrong with your dog?" Billy asked curiously, if not sheepishly.

"The dog won't come even if I call to him," Warren responded. "He stays there because of a spiritual encounter that scared him."

As they walked through the house, Ed pointed out the artifacts from the Warrens most prized investigations: a self-playing organ from the Amityville Horror, a demonically possessed Raggedy Ann doll from another case, a supernaturally shattered crucifix displayed in a see-through box.

Then he took Billy down to the basement. "Do not touch" signs had been placed throughout the house. Billy reached out to touch some artifacts.

"Don't touch that!" Warren screamed. "You'll unleash something here that even I can't deal with."

"Okay, okay," Billy said, feeling the hairs on his neck stand up. Billy fingered the holster holding his .357 magnum. "Mr. Warren, I can't stay down here in your basement, because I'll air-condition your entire basement if something down here moves." He had six rounds in the gun and two speed loaders. He would have blown out the entire place if something had moved.

They went upstairs. Billy went outside to make sure the arrow-happy perpetrators were not lurking about.

It was a calm night. No wind. Billy walked around looking and listening for something unusual. He saw nothing. He heard nothing. Then he walked over to his police car. Suddenly, a swift circle of leaves kicked up around Billy. With a quick-paced twister-like movement they surrounded him in mid air, going round and round. Except there was no one visibly there and there wasn't any wind. Billy freaked.

"Damn, what the fuck is this!" Billy shouted. He jumped in his car, turned on the ignition, and squealed off.

Later, confirming Billy's details of the evening, Ed and

Lorraine Warren explained that they had been victims of forces into black magic and satanism.

Ed Warren says, "Billy experienced a psychic cone of wind. People who are into black magic and satanism, they can project that kind of phenomenon. What Billy is talking about, Lorraine actually was picked up and thrown by an invisible force twenty-five feet and was hospitalized for almost a month. This is the kind of phenomenon that we, of course, encounter in our work that he would not, but he was about to encounter it. He could have been in danger had he stayed there.

"Someone was trying to harm us, so he was going to become what we call a soul victim. The strange thing is, when we go to Great Britain or when we're out of town, we ask the police to take a ride down the back of our property. They all laugh and say, 'Yeah, right, sure.' They never go down the back of the property. They don't feel much differently than Billy did."

For Billy the experience was like being a participant in a horror film. "A soul victim? That's what I was going to be? I'll take on drug dealers and killers and all kinds of crazy people, but I'm not into that ghost shit. The color of my skin is brown, but I turned off-color that night. Bullets can't stop that shit. I'm glad I ran."

Not only did Billy leave the Warrens' home, he would soon leave the Monroe Police Department altogether. The call he had waited for materialized. The City of Bridgeport's Civil Service Department informed him that he had made the cut for the city's new class of police recruits. Within weeks he would go from chasing stray animals and eerie visitors to chasing major drug dealers—alone and undercover.

CHAPTER 6

Bridgeport PD

JANUARY 11, 1984: Bridgeport Police Officers Fred DiNapoli and Frank DelToro were licking their chops.

DiNapoli and DelToro had waited a long time for this moment. They stood shoulder to shoulder in the lobby of Bridgeport Police Headquarters with their backs to the elevator that ran to the third-floor offices of the police superintendent. They barred the IN door against their long-time enemy: Bridgeport's feared and revered top cop, Joseph A. Walsh.

Walsh was the masterful survivor of an FBI sting attempt, survivor of two decades of fights with mayors and police board members who didn't like his style, a man who grimly battled officers he considered insubordinate with the same tenacity he battled criminals.

Earlier, Walsh had suspended DiNapoli and DelToro and transferred them to beats in the Bridgeport equivalents of Siberia. The pair had to fight Joe in court to regain equal treatment on the job. But this day was their time for revenge.

One month earlier, Walsh was at home nursing a blood clot in his leg when he was fired by Mayor Leonard S. Paoletta and the city's Board of Police Commissioners. Armed with a management study critical of Walsh's handling of the department, a history of bitter disputes, and a clause of dubious legality in the city's charter, Paoletta concluded Walsh was over the hill and ready for the push down.

Walsh said, "No way."

Walsh had appealed his removal to the city's Civil Service Commission and won reinstatement—or so he thought. On this day, hand in hand with his wife, Christine, and surrounded by police brass, supporters, and reporters, Walsh marched down the block from City Hall to police headquarters like a conqueror of Rome leading his troops to sack the Senate.

Instead, the police superintendent was heading to a showdown. He strode into the lobby of police headquarters. Standing in front of the elevator was a human wall, five hundred pounds of DiNapoli and DelToro. To the hundred people who witnessed the scene in the packed lobby it was as shocking as a fever's chills.

Walsh's reputation for getting his own way had earned him the nickname "Jaws," taken from the initials in his name. Now he stood in front of the two men. "Let me through," he thundered.

DiNapoli and DelToro were large, short-tempered, and powerful enough to bench-press the entire building. Fingers pressed holstered guns everywhere. It was more than just a fleeting thought that someone could be killed. Many years of fierce emotions were nose to nose as DiNapoli and DelToro stood dark-glassed, hair slicked back in their Seruchi jackets. They hated Walsh and Walsh hated them.

"I'm a sworn police officer, and on the orders of Mayor Paoletta you're not allowed on the third floor," DelToro told Walsh.

"Let me through," Walsh said again.

"On the orders of Mayor Paoletta . . . " DelToro repeated.

At this point former Superior Court Judge James Stapleton, Walsh's tall and big-boned lawyer and a long-time political enemy of Paoletta, shouldered forward, waving the commission's ruling in front of DiNapoli and DelToro. The two didn't budge. They weren't moving even if it meant spending the rest of their lives counting seagulls at the city dump.

The crowd's buzzing increased, photographers snapped pictures, television crews rolled their videotape. Defying the Civil Service's reinstatement of Walsh, Paoletta looked at the sixty-seven-year-old police superintendent, whose flushed face was inches away from his own.

"Joe," said the mayor.

"It's Superintendent to you," Walsh shouted back.

"I'm in charge of this department. I'm ordering you not to return to this office. Police officers will intervene."

Something had to give, and fortunately for the increasingly worried crowd, Stapleton's hushed advice convinced Walsh to do the sensible thing. There would be another day.

"See you in court," Walsh responded, leading his troops out of the building.

For DiNapoli and DelToro, this moment was like a mouse sticking out his middle finger to an eagle and living to tell about it. It was their shining moment in a career-long battle with Walsh.

Watching the Paoletta–Walsh standoff was an agonizing experience for members of the police department, pitting cop against cop, Paoletta followers against Walsh supporters. No one was neutral, or allowed to remain neutral. Every cop was forced to take a side. Controversy seemed to know no boundaries in the Bridgeport Police Department.

Most of it flowed from Walsh: cunning, charming, and charismatic, he was an old-style cop who liked to do things his own way. Tall and red-faced, Walsh had lost the pinky finger of his right hand in an encounter with an electric fan. The Boss, as he was also called, made it a habit of taking care of those loyal to him. Those who challenged him suffered long and hard. It was said of Walsh that he had an unflattering dossier on everyone he came in contact with. One thing was certain: To remind himself exactly what he thought of one enemy member of the board of police commissioners, Walsh kept a nicely carved-out oval portrait of the man affixed to the inside of his office toilet seat. Such touches were enough to keep some enemies at bay, others friends for life.

Walsh was born February 27, 1916, in a section of Bridgeport called The Hollow, a multi-housing neighborhood of working-class Irish and Italian immigrants. The youngest of ten children, his father died when Joe was four. He was the first cop in the department's history to graduate to the top job through the civil service testing system, which hires and promotes police officers based solely on written and oral examinations. Walsh earned praise as one of the department's finest officers, a detective who could figure out what phone number a person was dialing simply by listening to the dial turn. By the 1950s, he was celebrated throughout Bridgeport for his ability to crack difficult cases using his intuition into the criminal mind and a network of snitches in the community.

But what made Walsh a legend were the stories. For example, the story of the homeless, down-and-out cop-house custodian who appealed to Walsh for help. The superintendent gave the guy permission to make his home in the department's boiler room. Another Walsh story circulated about the fellow whose heart failed him while in bed with his mistress. Walsh directed his men to clothe the dead man and place his body on the sidewalk so his wife would

CHASED

think he'd been out on an early-morning stroll.

His reputation was enhanced during the hot summers of the 1960s when Bridgeport avoided the kind of racial violence that plagued other cities during the civil rights movement. Part of the calm was caused by tough talk and a willingness to back it up with tough action. Just that had resulted in many other cities burning; Joe Walsh, however, had a golden Irish tongue with which to talk, negotiate, and compromise, and wasn't opposed to letting his adversaries get away once in awhile.

There was a story about the time the police trapped members of a radical Puerto Rican group, the Young Lords, in an East Main Street tenement. The cops had them surrounded. The gang was ordered to surrender. No surrender. Tension was high. Would police burst through with guns blazing to face guns blazing? The police superintendent set a 5:00 A.M. deadline for surrender, publicly, on the street through a bullhorn and over the radio just in case someone wanted to be sure. Somehow, someway, the Lords snuck out of the tenement in the middle of the night and melted into the crowded East Side neighborhood. When the cops burst in at 5:00 A.M., there was no one there. It wasn't really a surprise; according to the story, the police sentries out back had been pulled. But honor had been maintained. The Lords hadn't surrendered and been humiliated; the cops had their raid and hadn't been humiliated in public. Everyone lived to fight another day.

It was a cardinal rule of the Bridgeport Police Department: if an arrest in a mob situation might cause a riot, postpone the arrest if police honor and community peace could be maintained or restored.

One hot summer afternoon in 1981, a woman got out of her car to protest when a gang on the corner of the notorious Father Panik Village housing project directed a deluge of water from a fire hydrant into her automobile. The mob assaulted her. A law-abiding citizen from a nearby apartment called police. The first squad car responding was ambushed by the mob. So was the second. So were the third and fourth. Each car drew more people like a magnet. Finally, the entire city shift ended up in the melée, and their only job was to pull the other cops out.

Somebody got into a cop's holster, swiped his revolver, and started firing into the air.

It was complete madness. Miraculously, no one was killed.

By the time things were sorted out, at least four police cruisers were trashed and eight police officers were in the hospital with injuries ranging from contusions to broken bones. The police captain in charge of the shift refused to let his officers back into the project to apprehend the perpetrators. The officers—black, brown, and white alike—were furious, and the assaulters were all black.

"We can't let them do this to us!" Ted Meekins, a huge black patrol officer, yelled directly into the face of his captain.

"We don't have enough men, and besides, it would just make things worse," said Captain Patrick Dolan, dripping with sweat, trying to keep his own cool with the insurrection erupting from his own bruised, cut, and disheveled officers.

It didn't make things better for those patrol officers on their feet to see their colleagues coming back to the patrol office bandaged and in arm casts. Yells at their captain were punctuated with obscenities. Still, Dolan didn't budge.

Upstairs in the Detective Bureau a month or two later the dispassion hadn't changed. "We'll get 'em on a cold night in February when their friends aren't around," explained then–Police Detective Fred DiNapoli to a police reporter one night.

And he did.

That was Joe Walsh's philosophy exactly. DiNapoli would rather choke on his linguine than admit that Walsh taught him a few things. But the tough old bird did rub off on DiNapoli in some ways.

This was Joe Walsh's police department.

Whatever allegations surfaced, Walsh rose from the clouds of

CHASED

dust as one of the shrewdest, most powerful politicians in Bridgeport. Despite this, the FBI had concluded that Walsh operated a crooked department in a wide-open town. He not only condoned corruption, they said, but was corrupt himself.

□   □   □

By the late 1970s and early 1980s, the U.S. Justice Department's Organized Crime and Racketeering Strike Force had several marching orders: Move in earnest against the entrenched operations of the Gambino and Genovese organized crime families. They did. Jail Hell's Angel Daniel Bifield, a man a federal probation report called one of the country's most dangerous men and a free-lance muscleman for the mob. They did. Bust up the labor racketeering in the local Teamsters Union. They did. Finally, get Joe Walsh. They didn't.

The feds achieved and received overwhelming praise for their massive crackdown on organized crime, gradually weeding out an element that thrived in one of the most wide-open mob cities in the country. Just how and why these men known as capos and soldiers had operated so freely sparked two very different law enforcement opinions. Joe Walsh always cited the lack of manpower and resources as his standard answer of the city police.

"We are handicapped," Walsh would say. "If I had the power to grant immunity, if I had unlimited manpower and money, the power to tap telephones, we'd have gotten these men at the top." The feds claimed the only thing lacking was enthusiasm for the task.

A clearer picture of how Bridgeport became a good place for the Mafia to do business emerges with examination of the Prohibition era. Connecticut was one of two states that did not ratify the Eighteenth Amendment, which prohibited the manufacture, sale, or transportation of intoxicating liquors. State lawmakers complained that such a law was an infringement on the rights of citizens.

Although the state was technically forced to abide by the federal law, Bridgeport law enforcement did little to enforce it. As a result, Bridgeport blossomed as a place where bootleggers could operate with little trouble. When Prohibition became law in 1919, the city had already earned its reputation as a hard-drinking, hard-fisted town. The patrons of the downtown speakeasies, many of them Irish, German, and Italian laborers, were not going to be deterred from their evening boilermakers by lawmakers in Washington. For drinkers who preferred privacy, there was always the option of making your own at home. It could be a messy chore, though, and ceilings splattered with home brew were not uncommon.

The more fastidious moved their stills to outdoor locations. A secluded, wooded area of Bridgeport developed into a noted haven and to this day retains the name "Whiskey Hill." Its remote stills were renowned for their quality, volume, and egalitarian sales practices. All customers, cops included, were welcome. But while cops were among the customers, there were appearances to maintain.

There were occasional raids. The city's press dutifully recorded the activities of the men in blue, but the reporters bought their booze up on Whiskey Hill, too. The boots always knew when the raids were coming; the cops told them. The reporters knew it, but there were appearances to maintain.

Not enough for U.S. Treasury agents. Eventually, they put a noticeable dent in the local traffic. As a rule, they did not inform local authorities of impending raids. They feared a connected cop would alert a friendly still operator, which did happen and continued to happen after Prohibition. As a result, isolation from Bridgeport Police became tradition among outside state and federal law enforcement officials.

What wasn't brewed locally was being smuggled. Whether by harbor or by hearse, liquor flowed through the city. Close to New York yet far enough away to provide some sanctuary, Bridgeport became attractive to men whose business practices occasionally drew the attention of law enforcement agencies.

There were scores of such "businessmen," but perhaps the most flamboyant and famous of them all was a man named Arthur Flegenheimer, better known at Dutch Schultz, the man U.S. District Attorney Thomas E. Dewey called the "biggest gangster" in New York City.

Bridgeport's reputation as a wide-open town was an invitation for guys like Schultz to visit even after the repeal of Prohibition in 1933. Schultz spent a lot of time in 1935 living at Bridgeport's Stratfield Hotel, where he played cards with cops, lawyers, and heavyweight businessmen who thought of him as something of a celebrity. For Schultz, Bridgeport was a pleasant place where he could avoid the persistent inquiries of federal authorities. But if Bridgeport had a reputation, it was nothing compared to Schultz's.

"Dutch Schultz has given the Bridgeport Police Department twenty-four hours to get out of town," wrote wisecracking *Bridgeport Herald* columnist Harry Neighor upon the gangster's arrival in Bridgeport. The last thing Schultz wanted in Bridgeport was trouble. He had plenty of that elsewhere. As it turned out, when Schultz left Bridgeport to watch the Max Baer–Joe Louis title fight at Yankee Stadium, federal authorities arrested him in New Jersey for tax evasion. About one month later, Schultz was blasted to death in a Newark, New Jersey, restaurant.

Decades before and after Schultz's visits to Bridgeport, wiseguys ran the city's rackets with little trouble. It was not until the late 1970s that their free rein in Bridgeport tightened up. Federal investigators Richard Gregorie, William Keefer, and John "The Bull" Durham turned up the heat. Armed with court-authorized wiretaps, they started closing in on the local operations of the Vito Genovese and Carlo Gambino organized crime families. In some cases, they didn't move fast enough. For example, someone eliminated the need to continue a federal grand jury investigation of Thomas "Tommy the Blond" Vastano, a Genovese soldier, by shooting him to death in his Stratford, Connecticut, backyard. Then two shotgun blasts disconnected Gambino capo Frank "Cigars" Piccolo in September 1981, while he stood at a public phone booth on Bridgeport's Main Street.

Strike Force investigations culminated with a number of Connecticut mob figures sentenced to double-digit jail terms. Whether it was federal authorities or inter-mob rivals concerned with preventing leaks by colleagues in the grand jury room, the combined zeal of these two organizations put a serious crimp in organized crime activities.

☐ ☐ ☐

The feds concluded that local cops had swept the underworld problems under the carpet. They set their eyes on Walsh and his longtime associate, Police Inspector Anthony Fabrizi, a balding, wiry, tough-as-nails Italian-American with a piercing, dark stare and a temper like a rattlesnake.

Outwardly, they were very different: Walsh the soft touch, the story-telling Irishman, cunning in his revenge; Fabrizi the fearless, sneering, in-your-face verbal attacker. "You don't like it, fuck you!" was a regular Fabrizi utterance to reporters or federal officials, just in case there was any question about where he stood. Whether going after bad guys or being labeled bad guys, together Walsh and Fabrizi were a formidable team. Between themselves, they fought persistently over issues in the police department, and although he would never talk about it openly, Fabrizi privately longed for the day Walsh would retire, allowing for his own ascension to the top of the police ranks. But when they had a common enemy, Walsh and Fabrizi bonded like Siamese twins.

On August 18, 1981, an event occurred that lit up the front pages of newspapers all over the world. It brought together the most powerful law enforcement officials in the country, including David

CHASED

Margolis, the chief of the U.S. Justice Department's Organized Crime and Racketeering Strike Force.

A towing contract had become an embarrassment to the city—too many towed cars were damaged under the custody of the Marra garage. Walsh was forced to take away the contract from Marra's family-run garage to silence community outcry and because Mayor John Mandanici wanted to derail the issue in an election year. Two months earlier, the feds had disclosed that both Walsh and Fabrizi were targets of a grand jury exploring possible violations of the Racketeer Influenced Corrupt Organization Act.

Thomas Marra, Jr., a colorful character, had earned a reputation as the Robin Hood of car thieves, ripping off luxury cars throughout the Northeast and selling them at bargain prices to the underclasses of the inner city. Marra's uncanny duplication of vehicle titles and registrations drove officials at the Connecticut Motor Vehicles Department mad and, in fact, forced them to amend colors and paper patterns to avoid counterfeiting.

Eventually, state and federal officials caught up to Marra. He was facing a thirty-year prison sentence on charges of first- and second-degree larceny and second-degree forgery for the sale of a stolen car. He had also been convicted in federal court in New Hampshire on charges of interstate transportation of stolen cars. With the hope of reducing his sentence on the New Hampshire conviction, Marra began working as an informer with the FBI.

FBI agents coached Marra through several trial runs before the actual encounter with Walsh. They provided him with a series of instructions: do not get into the car with Walsh; do not bring up the subject of money, let Walsh do that; if at any time the conversation with Walsh is uncomfortable, break off the conversation and abort. At 6:45 P.M. one evening, Special Agents Brendan Fisk and William Hutton escorted Marra to the downtown meeting spot where Walsh was scheduled to meet Marra at 7:15 P.M.

Little did the feds know, however, that while Marra wore a

concealed recorder, so too did Walsh. Happy, full of life, cracking jokes, Walsh crooned the tune "Little Things Mean a Lot," on his drive to the meeting spot. "I hope this thing is working," Walsh barked into his body recorder as he neared Main and Chapel, the meeting spot, a mere block and a half from police headquarters.

The scene was set, the participants in place. The feds staked out in a nearby van. Walsh's boys staked out in a nearby vacant firehouse.

"Come on, get in, lover," Walsh said to Marra, who obliged Walsh, breaking one of the feds' commandments.

"What the hell we got to do to straighten this towing out?" Marra asked.

"I don't know. I'm kind of in a bind. What do you suggest?"

"Joe, I got some money put away. I scraped up some cash. I got to give it back to my uncle. If we gotta, you know, go through you, through the mayor, through somebody."

"The mayor's not involved. I'm the one who runs it. Well, what are you offering?"

"I can come up with about thirty grand."

"Thirty grand? That sounds good. Okay. Let's understand. Let's lay it on the line now, and we'll work from there."

"Okay, I can give you some of the money now. When we get back the towing, I'll give you the rest, and keep coming up with a couple, whichever way you want to work it. You lay the line down with me."

"You're offering me thirty grand to change it back to the way it was so your old man would have the towing of stolen cars?"

"Right."

"Where's the money? How much you got with you?"

"Five, six thousand."

"It's a deal. I won't say it's a deal. We'll work it out. You trust me or what?"

"Yeah, I trust you. How soon can we get it back?"

CHASED

"Within a week, maybe?"

"Okay, take me to my car."

"I'll wait, you go."

Marra, having by now done exactly everything the feds told him not to do, went back to his car, picked up the money, and ignored the feds' beeping signal to abort the mission. By now, the feds smelled a rat.

"Should be five in there, Joe. Why don't you count it."

"I don't want to count anything, I trust you. Now put your hands on the dashboard; you're under arrest for attempted bribery! Don't move because if you run I'm going to fucking shoot you!"

Walsh's men moved in; the feds moved in.

Mass confusion and a tense standoff between two law enforcement agencies followed as FBI agents rushed to Marra's assistance. Walsh's men grabbed Marra, threw him up against the car, stripped him of his pants, and snatched the recording box from his leg. Special Agents Bill Hutton and Brendan Fisk demanded that Marra be released.

"He's coming with us."

"No, he's not."

"Yes, he is."

Walsh refused the agents' claims and ordered his officers to take Marra into custody. Gleefully snapping pictures of the laughable event was *Bridgeport Post* photographer Frank W. Decerbo, who had been tipped off by Walsh to watch from the sidelines.

U.S. District Court Judge T. F. Gilroy Daly dismissed the bribery charge against Marra, ruling that he was acting under the "behest, direction, and control" of federal agents and lacked criminal intent. Walsh emerged from the incident looking better than ever—a righteous hero ready to raise serious questions about sting-type law enforcement methods. For years, the feds had tried to catch him as a cop on the take; now he'd taken them. While Walsh gloated, embarrassed members of the U.S. Justice Department shuffled home looking like the Keystone Kops. The feds hadn't counted on the fact that Walsh was prepared for a set up.

What the feds had overlooked in their zealous pursuit of Walsh and Fabrizi was the duo's intuitive knowledge of human nature and of every single hood in the city, including Marra's family, who had known Walsh and Fabrizi for decades. While Walsh later maintained, "It didn't take a genius to figure out what was happening," Marra, prone to outrageous exaggerations, confessed later that the idea of stooging against a man he'd known all his life was too much for him, so he had gotten word to Walsh—something to this day Walsh denies.

However, not long after the sting, Marra would revert to his old car thief habits and later was returned to jail on state and federal charges.

In talking about that day, Joe Walsh says: "The attitude of the Strike Force was that the average policeman is on the take. Bag a chief—that was their attitude when they moved here. I was stunned. I laughed. I said, 'This is garbage. I've know the Marras since I was a rookie cop. Anybody that offers Joe Walsh money has got to be crazy.' I contacted Inspector Fabrizi, told him the whole story, and laughed about it. I said, 'If this guy offers me money he's going right in the can.'

"To make sure everything was lined up properly I called State's Attorney Donald Browne, and he told me I was crazy, that the government wouldn't do anything like this. I told him, 'I want you to know ahead of time that we are going to be prepared.' We knew Marra was an informant for the FBI."

After the botched sting attempt, the Bridgeport field office of the FBI had little to do with Walsh's department, except for the few cops it trusted implicitly, which were usually those who hated Walsh.

Mayor Paoletta placed Walsh in limbo in 1984 with his unilateral actions. It was up to the state Superior Court to decide Walsh's

C H A S E D

fate. As a reward for facing up to Walsh at the elevator, Paoletta promoted Fred DiNapoli to head the department's vice squad.

Into this hornet's nest Billy Chase stepped when he joined the Bridgeport Police Department.

CHAPTER 7

Fort Dicks

INITIALLY, BILLY WAS ASSIGNED to hit-and-run cases. He worked to clear up the department's huge case backlog, but Billy knew he wasn't meant for such tedious work—there was no action.

"I knew I could make a better contribution. Who knew the streets of Bridgeport better than me? I wanted to do Miami Vice shit. I knew I could be good at that."

Anticipating acceptance into the city's Vice Division, Billy didn't even bother purchasing a blue uniform for his police identification photo shoot. Standing in line with other rookies waiting to have their picture taken, Billy turned to Bob Koskuba, a recruit who joined the department with Billy.

"Hey, Bob, I don't have a uniform for my picture."

"Why not?"

"I just don't expect to be in uniform at all. Can I borrow your shirt and tie for this?"

Koskuba looked at Billy oddly, then smiled. Off came his tie and then his shirt. Billy had his photograph taken in borrowed clothes.

Next Billy began preparing a proposal to gain entry into Vice Division. He drew up the proposal like a business plan, focusing attention on the growing drug problem in the city, how his intimate knowledge of the streets would help eradicate the illegal narcotics trade, and how this would make the present administration and those in power look good.

"Give me a chance and I'll show you what I can do," Billy's proposal explained to Fred DiNapoli, who in his status as head of the Narcotics Division wanted passionately to swat the city's drug trade.

DiNapoli's vendetta against Walsh continued. He was as stubborn as they came when he believed he was right. And his partner, Frank DelToro, was of equal strength and tenacity: a not-to-be-messed-with tag team.

DiNapoli got his start on the Bridgeport Police Department in 1962 when he went undercover as a trick to nab a prostitute. In the late 1960s he worked in the department's Tactical Division during the city's Black Panther rioting, made numerous drug arrests and earned a reputation as a fearless cop. If his battles on the street were not tough enough, his fights with Joe Walsh turned into battles of epic proportion. DiNapoli became characterized as a stubborn and brash union leader who detested Walsh's equally stubborn and brash administrative style. DiNapoli spoke out against and picketed Walsh. Through the years, DiNapoli found himself walking the most unpopular beats in the city as a victim, he claimed, of retaliation. First it was the sewage plant, then the court house, then came Father Panik Village, one of the city's high-crime public housing complexes.

CHASED

As DiNapoli and DelToro faced the ghetto together, their bond against Walsh grew angrier and stronger. They spent eight or more hours together at work, and then beefed up their muscled bodies at the local YMCA. When they weren't at work, in the gym, or at home with their families, they'd attend many municipal board meetings—privately leaning on people to see it their way about Walsh and complaining to newspaper reporters of stories they thought were pro-Walsh.

Walsh, however, was not their only passion; fortunately, DiNapoli applied most of his fortitude to putting bad guys in jail. After years of bitter battles with Walsh and banishment to creatively designed beats to make their lives miserable, they finally had the upper hand. They now ran the police department. If Walsh had anything to say to DiNapoli or DelToro, it was like saying it to Paoletta. With the municipal election around the corner, DiNapoli saw something in Billy that led him to believe he could make Paoletta look good and also produce a dent in his war against drugs.

"At that time the drug problem was really busting out," Billy says. "Crack was just starting and people were blowing each other's brains out from the violent effect." DiNapoli cleared Billy's proposal with Paoletta. Billy was assigned to the Vice Department working with veteran undercovers Jack Flynn and Joe Hajducky, as well as Terry Sprankle, an investigator with the Drug Enforcement Administration.

On Billy's first day with DiNapoli, the tough cop didn't waste any time.

"Hey, kid, here's fifty bucks for some buys," he told Billy. "Show me what you can do."

A short while later, DEA Special Agent Bobby Graham handed Billy a law enforcement training book. The book included just two pages outlining law enforcement procedures and tips for undercovers.

"Good luck," Graham said.

Billy thumbed through the book. "This is it?" he asked. "There's no other undercover training in here?"

"Whatever is in the book," Graham said in a monotone.

Billy sighed. Improvise, adapt, overcome—these were Billy Chase trademarks. Now they would become even more important—his life would depend on them.

In his newly assigned position in the Special Services Division of the Bridgeport Police Department, he interfaced on a number of cases with federal law enforcement officials. Billy was a cop in Bridgeport, where advanced training was as common as a crimeless day. How does an undercover with no formalized training get started?

In Billy's case it was go where you know best—the streets. The best undercovers are those who are raised in the streets. Billy reconnected with the comings and goings of the streets of his youth, back to the inner-city playgrounds where he once shot hoops, into the strip bars and taverns that warehouse information about drug dealers, junkies, and prostitutes.

Maintaining a low profile would not be easy, but most of Billy's childhood contacts thought he had gone overseas to play basketball. When he stopped playing ball he also stopped associating with a lot of people from Bridgeport. He was in the working world, with no need to hang out in bars with old school chums. Just in case someone became suspicious, he arranged for a cover. Anyone who called the Monroe Police Department to ask about his whereabouts was told that he'd been fired and was out of law enforcement.

This worked to perfection with Billy's former mother-in-law, who had no use for him when he and his first wife split. She gleefully went around telling anyone willing to listen to her, "Chase is a loser. He lost his job. Good thing my daughter divorced him." Leave it to a former mother-in-law to expand someone's cover.

One potential sticking point was the city's residency requirement for city employees. Although a lot of city cops violated the

CHASED

rules, spending their personal time in suburban towns while maintaining an address in the city, the law said police officers were supposed to live in Bridgeport. Such a residence meant more opportunities to be recognized, more opportunities for Billy's cover to be blown. But he didn't want to make waves so early in the game. Worse yet, if some self-righteous cop filed a grievance against him, most likely it would be noted in the local press, and then his cover really would be blown.

So Billy took an apartment on the affordable East Side, not far from major drug areas.

Here the Dicks brothers were kings. Carl Dicks, Alfred Dicks, Danny Dicks, Angelo Dicks—so insulated that their heroin operation could have been called Fort Dicks. They controlled all of the heroin provided by the Gambino crime family in New York for the East Side of Bridgeport.

The Dickses were being supplied by mega heroin trafficker LeRoy Jackie Jackson, who owned the Star Dust Ballroom in the Bronx. Jackson was being supplied by Gene Gotti, the brother of Gambino crime boss John Gotti. This was about the time John Gotti was making his move to subvert Paul Castellano for control of the Gambino mob empire.

The Dickses had a legendary propensity for violence. If they wanted to send someone a message, they had three ways of taking care of the person's car: warning one, break the windows; warning two, set fire to the interior; warning three, blow it up with or without the victim inside. And just in case the person didn't get the message there was always Timothy Heartbeat, their New York–based enforcer. He was called Heartbeat, Billy said, because he'd kill people in a heartbeat.

So this was the dossier handed to Billy. Drug dealers, killers, and the Mafia—all in one little volatile package.

"The Dickses were booming, carrying some heavy shit," Billy says, "operating openly for years with little trouble, running drugs like it was legal, and making a ton of fucking money."

No one could touch them. The DEA had plenty of informants, but no agents clever enough to slip into the Dickses' operation. The Dickses were smart and they spooked easily.

Billy knew Carl Dicks from high school. The girl Dicks had dated and the girl Billy had dated were friends, and they had double-dated to the senior prom. One afternoon Billy ran into Carl Dicks at the Rite-Aid in Bridgeport. Recognizing each other, the two began talking.

"Yo, Carl, how ya been?"

"Hey, what have you been doing?"

"Ah, you know, I've been around, trying to keep busy. Say, I hear you guys have been booming over there, you're the man."

"Yeah, man, we're controlling shit over there. Things are going great."

"I got something going myself with some heroin with my cousin in Boston. What do you think, can I give you a call?"

Dicks gave Billy a phone number to call. Billy carefully put it in his pocket.

"I didn't know jack shit about heroin," Billy says. "I went to the DEA and told them that I was talking heroin with these guys but I was getting by on bullshit. Suppose they started asking me questions about cutting heroin? You sell heroin different than cocaine. You get quarters, sixty-five dollars apiece, for scrambled ounces. That means it's already cut, and you pay four or five thousand dollars. You could get a straight ounce of heroin that's uncut, for ten thousand dollars. A kilo of heroin costs two hundred and fifty thousand dollars. But you could cut that kilo seventeen times. I needed to know the language."

The DEA agreed. They sent him to the DEA training center in New York for a crash course in heroin street language. It was a strange kind of school, but it prepared Billy for some initial buys with the Dickses.

C H A S E D

Billy met Special Agent Terry Sprankle of the DEA and Jack Flynn and Joe Hajducky of the Bridgeport Police Department behind the Bridgeport Railroad Station for a briefing about the Dickses. Billy was fitted for a body wire, received marked buy money, and got into his car.

The Dickses' center of operations was Mr. D's, a dark and dank East Side bottle club that featured far more under-the-table drug buys than over-the-bar beer purchases.

Heading over to Mr. D's, the thought of doing serious undercover drug work in his hometown started sinking in. "Shit," Billy said, "I hope nobody makes me."

With his backup far in the distance, Billy pulled into the fenced-in parking lot of Mr. D's. He walked inside the bar and perched on a bar stool. Ordering scotch and water, he watched the comings and goings of people, black and white, escorted beyond the bar for certain back-room deals. He hailed the weasely faced bartender whose bloodshot eyes bespoke drug use.

"Where's Carl Dicks?" No response.

Billy got off the stool and repeated his question.

The bartender pointed to a swarthy tall man. "See my brother, Alfred. He'll take care of you," Carl Dicks told Billy, identifying his brother.

Alfred, a stocky sweating man, invited Billy to a quiet seat at the bar.

"I hear you guys have been really taking care of business," Billy said to Alfred.

"Yeah," Alfred said breathing heavily, "we're taking care of business."

"Can you hook me up with an ounce?"

A pregnant pause while Alfred looked him over. Alfred nodded, "Yeah, what do you need? A scrambled ounce is four grand, uncut is ten thousand."

"Okay, but right now I have five hundred dollars on me. Can

you hook me up with something?"

"No problem."

Alfred Dicks reached his beefy hand into his jacket. Beneath the bar he passed a bundle of bags containing heroin into Billy's hand. Billy breathed a sigh of relief. He was in. Dicks told Billy how they cut heroin, where they sold it, where they received it, and how many times Billy could cut what the Dickses sold him. While he spoke Dicks frothed at the mouth, and Billy, his heart racing, enjoyed every minute of it. This was what he joined the police for—not writing up traffic accidents, but making a dent in real crime.

The feds were happy with Billy's work, but they wanted a mega transaction before pressing charges. They asked Billy to set up an ounce buy under the supervision of the DEA. Billy arranged for a meeting at a shopping center in Stratford, just over the Bridgeport line.

The time was 4:00 P.M., which gave the feds a couple of hours to set up, wire Billy with a body transmitter, get the buy money, and settle in for the surveillance.

Everything seemed to be going smoothly. As Billy waited in the car, Alfred Dicks pulled his car along side.

"Yo, it ain't cool," Dicks said.

"What are you talking about?" Billy said, stunned by Dicks's announcement.

"It ain't cool." Dicks repeated.

While the feds were surveilling the area, the Dickses were doing their own surveillance, checking out the area before the feds had arrived. The Dickses' counter-surveillance observed the feds pulling into the area for a set up.

Billy bit his lip so he wouldn't curse out loud. The deal was blown. The Dickses pulled out.

"The Dickses weren't brainless gorillas," Billy says. "They set up their own counter-surveillance, and we learned a valuable lesson from that. If a drug dealer pulls into a parking lot to do a drug

CHASED

transaction and he sees a white man forty or fifty years old sitting in a car, it sends up an immediate signal that something's fucked up. It'll spook them.

"That's where the feds used to frustrate the shit out of me. If you're going to infiltrate a black operation you don't have a white guy sitting in the car. They're going to stick out like a sore thumb. Unless you have a white guy with a black guy, or a black chick with a white guy, you're not going to blend. Automatically they're going to know something's up."

Terry Sprankle from the DEA told Billy to reconnect with the Dickses. He called, but they did not respond. So he went to Mr. D's. When he arrived paranoia was rampant. Everyone was so cold Mr. D's could have been Mr. Death. The Dickses refused to see Billy. He decided to lay low and come back to them at a later time. If they didn't get busted, they might feel that everything was cool, that Billy probably was not a cop.

The botched sting against the Dickses was not a catastrophe. Billy had already made some hand-to-hand buys with Alfred Dicks, and the Dickses had introduced Billy to one of their key operatives, Leonard Jones. Now Jones escorted Billy to New York and gave him the scoop on how the New York connection operated. Jones introduced Billy to Jackie Jackson, who was being supplied by Gene Gotti. The DEA began turning up the heat on Jackson's New York operation. With Billy working the Dicks end and the New York feds working the Jackie Jackson end, the details of a massive criminal picture stretching from New York to Connecticut were emerging like a photograph soaking in a development tray.

In the next months the feds managed to flip Jackson into the Witness Protection Program. In return, he spilled his guts about Gene Gotti.

Then they got a federal indictment against key members of the Gambino crime family in New York City. The indictment outlined a criminal conspiracy that included Gene Gotti, the Dicks brothers, and Timothy Heartbeat, who alone was indicted on twenty-eight counts of murder.

Billy was brought to federal district court in Manhattan to testify.

On that Monday, the security in the Manhattan court building had never been tighter. Everyone was on edge. Billy prepared for his testimony in a chamber connected to the courtroom by a back entrance. As he prepared, his eyes swept the room. Suddenly Billy heard the rear door opening, followed by voices. He wheeled around. A man and a woman poked their heads into the room. When they saw Billy, they edged in the door, guns drawn. Billy pulled out his gun.

"Who the fuck are you!" Billy screamed.

"Who the fuck are you," the man and woman responded simultaneously, pointing their guns at Billy.

Just then, federal prosecutor Robert Hammel walked into the room. Three guns faced him.

"What are you people doing!" Hammel yelled. Then looking around, he laughed, "Now everyone relax. Billy, let me introduce you to two United States Marshals charged with keeping peace in the courthouse." Everyone sighed and holstered their weapons.

However, it was not the last tense moment. While Carl Dicks was on trial, Billy bumped into him at Main Port, a fish and chips place in Bridgeport.

"There's that fucking fed, Joe Fed. There's that motherfucker," Dicks shouted at Billy. The eatery was loaded with patrons who looked up from their fish sandwiches astonished.

"If you come any closer," Billy shot back, "I'm going to fuck you up today, so you can go over there and sit your ass back down or suffer the consequences."

Dicks stared at him for a long moment. "I'm gonna fuck you up some other day," Dicks replied, his voice steel-edged. "Count on it."

CHASED

Billy turned away and began eating his sandwich again. During his testimony, Billy linked the Dicks brothers with the Gambino crime family's New York drug operations. He named Gene Gotti and Angelo Ruggiero as the suppliers for Bridgeport. All were convicted.

CHAPTER 8

Sewers

"NOT THE SEWAGE treatment plant! Nothing could be worse than that," Billy growled when Roger Falcone, Billy's Vice Division supervisor, told him that he was being assigned to work undercover at the city's sewage treatment plant to investigate city employees who were suspected of dealing drugs on the job.

With the Dicks case behind him, Billy's newest undercover duties included surveying the disposal of waste matter drained away from houses, local towns, and factories. Bridgeport was famous for its regularly malfunctioning and stinking sewage treatment plant where raw sewage flowed freely into Long Island Sound. The antiquated plant suffered from a lack of city funds to modernize the facility. However, city residents suffered the most from the obnoxious odors that poured into the harbor and the unknown future consequences of the toxins.

The same budget problems that plagued the sewage plant also infected the city Police Department.

"Bridgeport was in bad fiscal condition, and our unit was underfunded," Billy says. "This was 1986 and the city provided me a 1963 Star Fire with the horn in the glove compartment as part of my cover. The car was buried in the city yard with a bunch of other jalopies. I looked like a black version of Columbo. What a job. I was undercover and underground."

As his cover, Billy used a story that he had just been released from the Navy, attended college by night, and worked for the city by day.

The sewage plant contained huge pipes the size of oil tankers that were driven by a lever that released all the sludge out into tanks. Turning the lever to the right could cause a flow build up and force the pipes to blow—a sludge bomb in the making.

"The plant employed this pothead who regularly came back from lunch all fucked up and hadn't a clue about what to do," Billy said. "We became friendly and he was an unwitting informant about the drug transactions that took place at the plant. But he was always fucked up on the job and this caused a number of problems for me. On one of my first days he asked me what to do. Now, I didn't know what the fuck I was doing either, so I told him to turn the lever to the right."

Fortunately Tom Sullivan, a white-haired supervisor, saw what was about to happen.

"Don't turn that!" he screamed. "One bit further to the right and we're all dead."

"What's wrong?" Billy inquired.

"If that pipe bursts, we'll all be buried in shit."

The plant also contained a room where workers prepared a lime mixture in huge vats that filtered down into a machine that dried the

CHASED

sludge and held it together until it was rolled out onto a conveyor belt and into a truck for disposal. The machine was supposed to drip excess mixture to prevent a backup.

On a day when nearly everyone else was out to lunch, this machine was left attended by "Mr. Pothead"—unattended would be more like it. When Billy returned from lunch the sewage plant was like Niagara Falls.

"Holy shit!" Billy shouted. "You let the vat back up."

Racing up the stairs toward the runaway vat Billy slipped on the lime mixture, which had a slimy soap-dish-like texture. He bounced on his bottom, slid across the floor and past the vat, and his head smashed against the wall. Semi-conscious, he climbed groggily to his feet. He looked like he'd spent a few cycles in a washing machine. He walked out into the freezing cold, soaking wet, slimed into his city jalopy, and drove home for a change of clothes.

The next day he came back for more.

The sewage treatment plant had a steep metal staircase. Every time plant workers left the room they hosed off the slippery liquid from their boot bottoms. Billy hadn't thought about this. He hit the first step and bounced down the entire staircase to the concrete floor, thirty steps, all the way on his back.

"I was fucked up. I couldn't move. I stumbled into the hospital to get some attention. But I had had enough of that sewage treatment plant. The next day I went into work, hooked up with one of the dealers, and made a coke buy."

Two sewage treatment plant employees were fired by the city as a result of Billy's undercover work. His next assignment was working undercover at the *Bridgeport Post*, the city's daily newspaper.

Bridgeport Post publisher Betty Pfriem contacted the Police Department about an employee working out of the paper's composing room suspected of supplying reporters with drugs. The police arranged for the paper to hire Billy to work in the maintenance department.

"This was one of the great challenges of undercover work, keeping your boss happy in your undercover job while doing your real job of nailing the other guy for dealing drugs. The only person at the *Bridgeport Post* who knew about me was Betty Pfriem. My immediate supervisor at the *Post* only knew that I was sweeping floors for him. He hadn't a clue about anything else. When he sent me out to clean, I had to find a way to keep him happy without him getting suspicious about my real goal. So I had to find a way to get my job done, run over there and deal with the suspected employee, put on the voice-activated tape recorder collecting the conversation I had with him, find a place to hide to write down my notes, stick them in my pocket, finish my job, and go home."

Billy wanted out of this undercover assignment real fast. Especially after he was handed a mop and told to clean the toilets. But by then he had a dossier on the guy, and didn't waste any time.

"Hey, what's up. Don't you remember me, we got hooked up before? The stuff was pretty decent."

"Oh, yeah, I remember."

"You think we can hook up again?"

"Yeah, yeah."

Billy made a number of exchanges and then the arrest.

Bigger and more important jobs came his way. In 1986, Connecticut Governor William O'Neill formed the Governor's Action Committee on Drug Education, which took a wide-ranging look at how the state—from the classroom to the courtroom— should combat Connecticut's growing drug scourge. Bridgeport's new mayor, Thomas W. Bucci, served as the chairman of the group, which included heavyweight political and elected officials such as U.S. Attorney Stanley Twardy. A task force comprised of local, state, and federal law enforcement agencies was formed in southwestern Connecticut in conjunction with the governor's drug plan.

CHASED

Billy was assigned to the task force.

He immediately engineered such a huge caseload, working around the clock without overtime pay, that the statewide Narcotics Division had to hire an extra secretary to keep up with the paperwork.

"Lois Lane couldn't type fast enough to keep pace with the paperwork," Billy said. "They brought in a secretary to transcribe my tapes and help prepare my reports. When I was in Bridgeport I had to do all my own undercover shit plus transcribe tapes on every case that I did. It was time consuming and tiresome, and it constantly bogged me down. I remember those days—that machine with the foot pedal. I had enough tapes to fill a storage room."

Not only were big-time numbers demanded, they pushed Billy to work on cases no one else would—or should—do. He didn't know it, but he was preparing himself for the biggest drug case in the history of Connecticut. The Number One Family.

Billy's reputation as being fast, sharp, and quick to learn was growing within the ranks and outside them.

CHAPTER 9

The Number One Family

ST. ANTHONY'S ROMAN CATHOLIC CHURCH was a tiny retreat of prayer and peace serving a predominantly Latino community in the West End of Bridgeport.

The second generation Hungarians began to move out of the neighborhood and its cold-water flats, tenements, and multi-family houses on crowded streets for the more spacious status of suburban life.

In real-world cities like Bridgeport, a shot-and-beer town trying desperately to reconnect with its industrial past, the undercurrent of drugs had begun to destroy lives, street by street, block by block, leaving behind a chilling trail of blight, killings, and tragedy. For many inner-city kids examining employment choices, flipping hamburgers at McDonald's couldn't match the lure of standing cover for ruthless drug kingpins dangling crisp one-hundred-dollar bills and sparkling jewelry in their eyes.

No one better symbolized this insanity, the formidable drug problem, and the disdain for authority than Mariano Sanchez. He built a ruthless drug machine that scared the daylights out of the West End of Bridgeport. Sanchez patterned his inner-city street gang after traditional Mafia families. He was the capo, the head of the organization, who controlled all of the illegal drug activity through a team of lieutenants, soldiers, and associates, who in turn used people's bodies as collateral against snitching. They were number one and let everyone know it, modeling "The No. 1 Family" logo on jackets that Sanchez purchased for his members.

But those who knew Mariano saw him as an engaging, charismatic young man from the West End. He was more like Robin Hood, selling dope to wealthy suburban kids entering his turf and spreading his wealth among the needy neighborhood people, young and old, buying their everlasting loyalty and friendship, all with a smile. They called him "Boss."

"Mariano was a brilliant businessman," Billy said. "He treated the guys who worked for him very well. He'd buy them cars, take care of them and their families financially. The money gave him all the power he needed. The day Mariano made his first million he went down to Seaside Park and threw thousands of dollars out of the car window in celebration."

In good times and bad, for the decent, church-going people of the West End there was always St. Anthony's—for prayer, guidance, hope, and the inspiration that tomorrow might be better than today. And there was Father Nick Villamide, the nimble door-to-door priest, and the compassionate Monsignor Francis Campagnone, the pastor of the church—always available, always willing to listen.

One November afternoon in 1986, Father Villamide was driving through the neighborhood on his way back to the church. As he

CHASED

approached the church driveway, ready to pull into his parking space, a gang of young men blocked his way.

"What is the trouble?" the priest asked. Disdainful laughs returned his way.

"What, are you kidding?" they replied. "We own this neighborhood. We do business here. Your parking lot, too. There's nothing you can do about it. *We're* making the neighborhood better, not you."

For ten minutes they taunted Father Villamide with laughter, repulsive gestures, and reminders that they, not he, were in control. Finally, they allowed the humiliated priest to squeeze through. Father Villamide was the kind of street priest who'd knock on doors at night to stay in touch with his local parishioners. He was familiar with the rigors of inner-city clergy work, having spent ten years at an East Harlem, New York, parish before coming to Bridgeport. But what he encountered in Bridgeport was nothing like what he had experienced before.

"They think they have taken over this neighborhood and can do whatever they want," lamented Father Villamide. "The best people we have are moving. We want to fight the evil ones. We want our neighborhood back."

On another November afternoon, Monsignor Campagnone faced similar humiliation. Appealing to the decency of the drug dealers, hopeful that respect for the church could, in some way, convince the gang members to move on, he was scorned, ridiculed, laughed at. The drug dealers held eggs up high in front of his face for the monsignor to see, then pelted the space at his feet with a fury of flying eggs, the splatter kicking up on his shoes and pants. Other times, they intentionally blocked the driveway leading to the church parking lot, glaring and daring the monsignor to run them over.

It became clear that even the sanctuary of the church could not deflect the gang members' menacing disdain for authority. Any neighborhood person who dared confront these street-level dealers were mocked, laughed at, and pushed around with promises of retaliation if anyone complained.

And retaliate they did.

Helpless citizens were regularly roughed up, battered, beaten, shot at. The most vocal ones were murdered. One neighborhood resident made the mistake of confronting drug pushers—they silenced him with bullets.

"The criminals lock decent people in their own homes," said Monsignor Campagnone. "The parishioners are very quiet and fear repercussions. Even us at the church, we don't know if a bomb will come our way."

The monsignor was torn, though, because he knew the families of gang members. He had even baptized Mariano Sanchez's step brothers, so he hesitated calling the authorities. But the terror worsened.

"We're prisoners in our own homes. They've taken over completely," he said. Every day he looked out the window of his church. Gang members sold drugs openly, turning the streets into a supermarket for buyers. "I can't even drive out of my driveway, the traffic is so heavy with kids from suburban towns coming here to buy drugs."

Finally the monsignor called the police—but to no avail. "They kept telling us there was not much they can do." On the Fourth of July, the monsignor watched as gang members shot guns instead of fireworks. He called the police about the noise.

"Father, it's just some kids and fireworks," he was told. Monsignor Campagnone stuck the phone out the window, so the cops could hear the gunfire.

In 1984 Mariano began to traffic cocaine in the city's West End. He quickly organized a network of mid-level lieutenants and distributors, primarily members of his family or close associates, who packaged and distributed cocaine to and collected from some fifteen street dealers who sold directly to the public—insulating him from direct involvement in the day-to-day operations of his organization, but remaining responsible for obtaining the cocaine ultimately distributed by his street dealers.

Mariano and his crew used beepers and mobile telephones to conduct their drug transactions and often traded beepers and cars. Mariano alone was pulling down more than half a million dollars a year pushing cocaine from the city's West End. And he lived high. Enjoying her husband's success, Mariano's wife, Elsa, purchased her father a 1987 Cadillac for $29,000 in cash.

Mariano also lived the good life as a frequent visitor to Atlantic City, where he gambled large amounts of money and received first-class complimentary rooms. In 1986, he visited Harrah's Marina Hotel and Casino at least nine times, wagering a total of $123,000 and losing most of it. In the first quarter of 1987, he visited Harrah's sixteen times, wagering another $183,000. During those years Harrah's gave Sanchez complimentary rooms, transportation, and other items valued at nearly $35,000.

"Anytime homeboy felt like going to Atlantic City, they sent him a plane to fly him there, or sent a limo," Billy says. "He had a lot of respect in Atlantic City. He'd airdrop money like it was water."

To throw off any potential police surveillance, Mariano moved quickly and generally did not use his personal residence to store or cut the cocaine. By 1985 Mariano's organized army of drug warriors had made the West End of Bridgeport their headquarters. Gang members murdered with little motivation, frightened working-class citizens, and bought off kids to stake out street corners.

The clergy at St. Anthony's had two choices: do nothing and try to survive, or seek help.

"We've got to do something," said Monsignor Campagnone. He started a petition that hundreds of parishioners and people living in the vicinity of the church signed. It demanded action against the Number One Family. Monsignor Campagnone and Father Villamide sent the petition to the mayor's office and followed it up with a personal appeal to Mayor Thomas Bucci, who had won the mayoralty away from Leonard Paoletta. "Mayor, we need your help with this gang," Father Villamide told Bucci. "They are out of control and our parishioners are scared."

The Bridgeport Police Department's Vice Division had its eye on Mariano, but he was too well insulated, slick, smart, and had one potent weapon: cops in the department who were on his payroll.

Respect for clergy meant something to Bucci, much more than the usual tokenism politicians grant to the pious. The mayor was from a working-class background himself. He had grown up in the rough Hollow neighborhood, an incubator of sinners and saints for generations in Bridgeport. The mayor was educated in Catholic schools and proud of it. It wasn't political patter but genuine respect when he talked about his upbringing and the role of the Church in providing values, discipline, and family structure. He was a weekly communicant at church. His own children were educated in Catholic schools for the same reason.

Tom Bucci believed he could engineer social changes in government, and he became the first white politician to try it in Bridgeport. He recognized that African-Americans and Latinos, by the sheer force of their growing numbers, could no longer be ignored. They were demanding equal participation in political affairs. Bucci concluded that they must be accommodated, and not just with lip service.

He began appointing blacks and Latinos to government. This did nothing to endear Bucci to the political dinosaurs used to carving up the spoils in his Democratic Party. But then, most of them didn't have the votes anymore anyway.

Bucci's characteristic puns and openness with the media made him a favorite with the local press, which was fed up with years of

CHASED

confrontations with Mandanici and Paoletta. Bucci rarely imposed his will on anyone, preferring to govern by consensus. His sense of fairness and social equality rubbed off on aides and won him the respect of Bridgeport's press and progressive leaders, particularly the black and Latin clergy. So when the clergy representing African-American and Latin interests asked for help, his ears perked up like radar.

Because of his affirmative action program, Bucci had developed a special relationship with Bridgeport's minority community. Italian-American mayors of the past had generally stuffed cotton in their ears when the African-American and Latino communities spoke. It was always just easier to ignore them. They don't register, and those who do generally don't vote—that was how most white politicians characterized the minority community. But Bucci looked around the city and realized what had passed by others. Bridgeport was now basically one-third white, one-third black, and one-third brown.

By choice, Bucci had carved out his voter base in the following order: black, brown, white. It was by choice because the more attention he paid to blacks and Latinos, the more the old-time European-Americans pulled away. "He gives the blacks and Puerto Ricans everything," snarled many a power-hungry white politician. As a result, Bucci watched his white support wane, which meant he had to solidify his black and brown voter base even more.

Bucci savored his relationship with the minority community. His popularity was something no other Bridgeport mayor had enjoyed. He went to their churches, attended their festivals, and became educated in their cultures. *"Alcalde! Alcalde!"* the Latinos would shout at Bucci, the Spanish word for mayor, with an affectionate ring that fed Bucci's ego.

So when Father Villamide and Monsignor Campagnone called for his help, Bucci decided to make a personal appearance at the church to meet with the clergy. On this day, driving around the

West End, Bucci did not see the criminal activity the church parishioners were experiencing. The streets were quiet. Still, he believed the churchmen's words. During his meeting with them, Bucci agreed to organize a joint church rally to hear neighborhood concerns and mobilize local law enforcement officials as part of an anti-drug crackdown. Police Superintendent Joseph Walsh, who was there, promised more arrests. Bucci promised to beef up police presence, but residents complained that would not be enough. They were right.

Standing at the back of the church listening to the complaints and pleadings for help were ten defiant members of the Number One Family. Dressed in identical black suits and white shirts with ties, dark sunglasses shading their eyes, one of them, a swarthy-faced man, yelled out, "What are you going to do about us?" They taunted, they mocked.

"See things our way," a young, lean, black-haired gang member spat out. "We're doing more to help the people than you are."

In front of priests, the police superintendent, and the mayor the gang members were saying, "We're the people you're complaining about and you can't do a thing to stop us."

Just minutes after the meeting ended, the gang members brazenly walked into the church bathroom and dropped several packages on the floor. Some contained cocaine. Other packages contained human feces. As they left, the men once again laughed in the face of Father Villamide.

"It was the gang members' way of saying, 'To heck with you.'" Monsignor Campagnone shook his head.

The evening's events convinced Bucci that an unprecedented local, state, and federal law enforcement effort would be the only way to eradicate the Number One Family.

"I was enraged at what I saw," Bucci says. "I had confidence in the ability of government to handle this gang. This was a dramatic manifestation of what the drug epidemic was bringing to this community, a total disrespect for public officials, and disrespect for traditional religious authority and values. Threatening the life of Father Villamide, thumbing their noses at all of those institutions that were the fabric of whatever social consciousness the community had. The old rules no longer applied. This was the worst state of affairs."

Bucci had a special problem, however. He had aligned himself with Joe Walsh during the top cop's feud with the former mayor Leonard Paoletta and restored all of Walsh's powers after he was elected. Bucci knew that it would be impossible for the inflexible Walsh to rekindle his relationship with local federal law enforcement officials, many of whom were involved in the bungled sting attempt against Walsh.

Walsh was much too set in his ways, and the feds were too cynical, even if Walsh had tried to reach out. Bucci also knew that the restoration of the West End depended upon a renewed relationship between local and federal police. The mayor got on the phone without Walsh's knowledge. He arranged a meeting with U.S. Attorney Stanley Twardy, Paul Salute, head of the Bridgeport office of Connecticut's Drug Enforcement Administration, and members of the Bridgeport field office of the FBI.

Through the Police Department's Office of Internal Affairs, the one arm of the department that reported directly to the mayor, Bucci received word that some members of the city's Tactical Division in the Police Department had been bought off by Mariano.

"We can't take this drug gang out by ourselves," Bucci told Twardy, whom he had met through the drug task force created by Governor William O'Neill earlier that year. "I need your help. This gang is beyond the expertise of local law enforcement. We don't have the expertise, equipment, or the manpower."

In front of some twenty federal agents, Twardy guaranteed Bucci that his office would unleash an all-out law enforcement assault on the Number One Family, combining federal cooperation with the Statewide Narcotics Task Force to which the Bridgeport Police Department had assigned two of its members.

"The mayor sent a strong signal that he didn't care about the political consequences in the Police Department, he wanted to clean up the city," Twardy says. "In a second meeting we met with Walsh and made a tense situation do-able. A confluence of the elected mayor's office, the quasi-independent police chief, and federal law enforcement working together."

Through most of 1986, Billy Chase had been working in the Special Services Division of the Bridgeport Police Department. Under the rules of the Bridgeport Police Union, any promotions in police division had to be filled according to seniority. With only two weeks on the job in 1985, Billy had received entry into the division by Fred DiNapoli, bypassing union regulations.

DiNapoli was no longer around. Rather than face the restoration of Walsh's power, DiNapoli had retired just days after Paoletta lost the election to Bucci. Possibly jealous over his unorthodox rise, senior officers now filed a grievance about Billy.

Bucci, an expert in labor and union law and civil service procedure, had to make a decision about how to deal with the pending grievance. He knew if he let the grievance run its course, Billy would have surely been pulled out of the Vice Division and put back into Traffic, jeopardizing his undercover career and removing the department's top undercover agent.

Meanwhile, Bucci had agreed to assign two cops to the Statewide Narcotics Task Force. He was aware of the success Billy had achieved in working undercover at the *Bridgeport Post*, the Sewage Treatment Plant, and in nailing the Dicks brothers.

The decision was made: At the urging of Roger Falcone, the new head of the city's Vice Division, Bucci assigned Billy Chase and his close friend, Officer William Perez, to Statewide.

"There were no restrictions on whom I could assign to Statewide," Bucci says. "This gave me the ability to protect two of our

CHASED

own from being pulled out of the Narcotics Division while fulfilling the need to participate in Statewide."

Billy's career entered a whole new dimension. He was still a cop employed by the city, but he was given star status—he now worked under the authority of the State Police and federal law enforcement agencies.

Since the story naming him an undercover in the *Bridgeport Post* appeared, Billy worried that a number of drug dealers were on to him. He worried, but that didn't stop him. Nothing could.

CHAPTER 10

Broken Family

On a cold winter's night in 1987, a drug enforcement SWAT team planned a little surprise for Edward "Big Red" Giusti. The task force trying to nail Mariano Sanchez crashed the South End home of Mariano's key lieutenant and fourteen of his associates in a massive raid on Mariano's organization. One by one, a collection of local, state, and federal agents barged into Giusti's house and turned his belongings inside out, hopeful that some small piece of evidence—a trace of drugs, a ledger, a scale—could be used to squeeze information out of Big Red and lead them closer to Mariano.

As the evening hours passed on, the cops examined every room, every potential hiding place, every crack in the wall. The more the cops snooped around, the more their frustration intensified. Giusti's house was clean. So too were the fourteen other locations they searched. Every place came up dry. The cops on the scene started whispering their suspicions to each other; one more time, Mariano had made them look like the Keystone Kops.

Big Red was all smiles that evening as he watched the faces of the zealous cops lose their fizzle like a flat soft drink. Then Giusti set his eyes for the first time on Billy Chase, who was mingling among the disappointed undercovers. Giusti's glee turned to shock.

"You're a cop?" Giusti queried Billy.

"So what?" Billy answered.

Giusti shook his head, a perplexed look on his face. "Shit, you look just like somebody else, if you take that earring out."

Billy couldn't figure out who it was that he resembled. Could it be a drug dealer? Must be, to earn that look from Giusti. As everyone filed out of Giusti's house empty-handed, no further along in their quest to nail Mariano, Billy weighed his exchange with Giusti. Who knows? Looking like a drug dealer that Mariano had confidence in might help some day. He filed away the information.

"The Number One Family was all anyone would talk about," Billy says. "The guys Mariano had working for him were flamboyant. You knew who was down with Mariano. They all had their Number One Family jackets. But Mariano's army had insulated him; you couldn't touch him, no hand-to-hand buys. The Number One Family ruled.

"The key to Mariano's success was that he wasn't a user. Like the saying in the movie *Scarface*, 'Never get high off your own supply.' Drug dealers learned a lot from that movie about what can happen as a result of indulgence. Mariano was a good businessman. The only thing you would see people give him was money—never any drugs. Ralphy Villegas and Billy Perez really busted their ass trying to get him.

"Mariano had the best cocaine going. His connection was in Miami, and they were bringing it in by planes, trains, and

C H A S E D

automobiles. He'd mix it up. He was consistently inconsistent. Mariano had mules working for him, people who would carry the shit for him, men and women, for X amount of dollars. Everybody was working for Mariano—even cops. He had a police roster with names, phone numbers, and addresses of Bridgeport cops. *I* didn't even have a police roster."

Phone taps, body recorders, painstaking surveillance, sharing information, courage, and control are the markings of quality police work. Investigations take months, sometimes years of work, but even with all the law enforcement cooperation created through a common enemy, it doesn't hurt to have some old-fashioned luck.

On March 27, 1987, Mariano Sanchez's luck—and life—would change forever. That evening Billy in his undercover car loaded with police gear—radio, handcuffs, and work notes—was driving down the highway on his way home from karate school when he spotted Mariano's red Mazda RX7. Mariano stared at Billy. Intuitively, Billy placed his finger alongside his nose, a signal used on the street indicating his urge to buy some cocaine. Mariano acknowledged Billy's message with a wave to pull over. As Mariano emerged from his vehicle and walked toward Billy's car, Billy furiously shoved all evidence of police work under the seat. "If he sees this stuff," Billy murmured, "I'm dead."

Remembering the unintentional tip from Mariano's lieutenant, Big Red, Billy pulled off his earring. He rolled down the car window.

"Hey, what do you need?" Mariano asked, looking down at Billy.

"Can you hook me up with an ounce?"

"I'm waiting for something to come in now. It's going to take me a little time. Give me a call."

Mariano gave Billy his car phone number and told Billy to call him in an hour. Then he drove away. Exhilarated, Billy called Bridgeport detectives Billy Perez and Ralphy Villegas—they were the experts on Mariano. "Let's meet at the PD." When he got there, Billy called the car phone number. A man answered but explained that he couldn't talk.

Billy looked over at Villegas.

"I don't know if that was Mariano," Villegas said. "I'm not sure you had him on the phone."

Billy called Mariano again the next day. The man who answered the phone set up a meeting with Billy at Spanky's Arcade in Bridgeport. Perez and Villegas still weren't sure they had the right man.

"It was Mariano, it had to be Mariano," Billy appealed to Perez and Villegas, who shrugged their shoulders unassuredly.

"Let's take all precautions as if it is him," Billy insisted. On the chance Mariano would show up, everyone—DEA, FBI, State Police, undercover vans—pulled together for the meeting.

When Billy and the others arrived at the arcade, Mariano was there with one of his boys playing video games. The agents waited outside.

Coolly, assuredly, Billy sauntered in. Only he felt the cold clamminess of his hand, and he wiped it on his chinos. He walked straight up to Mariano. Mariano pointed at his henchman. "No," Billy said, glancing at the punk disdainfully. "I don't want to deal with anyone but you."

Mariano smiled wryly.

Quickly Billy went on—he didn't want Mariano to suspect anything. "Hey, you're the man, but I know the cops are watching you and I don't want to get jammed up with the cops."

"No one can touch me," Mariano said confidently. "Don't you worry about that. Just a few days ago I told a couple of them, 'I make more money in a week than you make in a year. Why don't you come work for me?'"

Billy met his eyes, "I hear a couple of them took you up on your offer."

CHASED

Mariano smiled wryly again but said nothing.

Billy took out a roll of bills and began to peel them off. Billy reflects on the scene: "I paid Mariano, and his buddy gave me the shit. Even if Mariano didn't give me the cocaine, he was there, he authorized it, so now we're rolling. We got it on tape and had video cameras rolling. The feds and state were all pumped up. They turned up the heat, received approval for phone taps and stepped up the surveillance. I felt like I had won Mariano's confidence; we were sort of comrades."

Billy still was unaware of the drug dealer Mariano had confused him with. Who cared? Things were working. Billy set up another buy at Waldbaum's supermarket. On May 23, he was parked in the Waldbaum's lot with just about every means of communications available—body monitor, police radio, car phone.

"If Mariano wants me to follow him, I'll proceed," Billy told his surveillance team, "but if he goes anywhere near the State Street area, I'll pull off." Mariano had his base of operations along State Street, an area where Billy could be spotted by people in Mariano's operation who knew him.

Anticipating that Mariano might jump into his car, Billy killed the switch on the police radio so that Mariano couldn't hear the transmissions between the other vehicles. Sergeant John O'Leary from the State Police and Roger Falcone, Billy's boss in Bridgeport PD, were his tail.

At 9:00 P.M. Mariano showed up in his bright red Mazda. Mariano rolled down the window. "Follow me," he said.

Billy notified his surveillance team. "Call me on the car phone if there's a problem with my following him."

Billy looked around. There were ten surveillance cars. There was so much noise going on between cars talking back and forth that O'Leary and Falcone had cut off their car radio. That was okay, because Billy knew they could still hear him on the body transmitter radio. Billy headed over to Maplewood Avenue. Mariano pulled over, got out, and hopped into Billy's car.

"It was cool the other night. I was chill," Billy said, adroitly trying to put the drug kingpin at ease and catch him off balance.

"Yeah, in places like Burger King, different places are bad to go to," Mariano replied, alluding to his meeting spots.

Billy's voice was eager, upbeat. "Yeah, I got these people up in Hamden and shit."

Mariano watched him closely. "Oh, yeah?"

Billy nodded. "Like you say, I'm making money hand over fist. How much can I get a pound for?" Billy asked.

"Hey," Mariano shrugged his shoulders, "I'll have to give you a price on that next time we see, 'cause I'm trying to negotiate with some other people and shit. I'll be getting it cheaper, so I'll give it to you cheaper."

"Oh, that'd be nice," Billy said nonchalantly.

Mariano relaxed a little bit and became more chatty. "'Cause right now like a lotta people fuckin' up—they kinda messin' up the business."

Billy wanted more details. He pressed a little. "You ain't getting paid, or what?"

Mariano kept on talking. "Yeah, a lotta people are competing against me. So what they'll do in order to try to make some good money is they go out there and they start talkin' to like the people who buy from us and they say, 'Well, how much does Mari give for you this?'"

Billy interrupted. "And then they undercut you and shit." Billy dangled a bit of bait.

Mariano bit it. "And then they say, 'Well, we'll give it to you.'"

"Yeah?"

Mariano's ego took over now. "See, but they don't know that I treat my customers so good, then they come back and say, 'Man, you know what I see today? He'll give it to me cheaper, but I'll stick with you.' And they're doing that. So what they do is, they

CHASED

fuck it up for them, and you know they don't care—no matter what, gonna come to me. And I always try not to come up, 'cause when the price goes down on me then I can do it on them and shit. I always try to do that. Yeah, but a lotta people mess it up."

It was the first important glimpse into Mariano's operation. Billy wanted to know more, but he knew he had to be careful. He chose his words cautiously.

"My boy came down here. He was over on the East Side or somethin', and that motherfucker that drives, that cop that drives that white Vet."

Billy waited.

"Dailey," Mariano said.

Billy smiled, "Fuckin' stopped him. Is he cool or what?"

Mariano nodded, "Yeah, see, like, if he don't know you he won't be cool, see, but like he's alright, you know, concerning the people that he knows."

Damn, Billy thought, *a crooked cop.* "Right," he said matter-of-factly.

Mariano went on. "You know, he knows who does this and this, but if he were to ever stop like say me, and then he got somebody that's lower than him in the car, I don't even have to worry about it. But if he's with somebody that's higher . . . you know, he don't check with us anyways 'cause he's cool, you know, he chats with us, but you know, if he ever has to do his job one day, you know, you can't blame him."

"Yeah, 'cause, you know, he gave my boy a hard time."

"He did?"

"Yeah."

"Where's your boy from?"

Billy paused then he said, "Well, he ain't from here."

Mariano smiled. "That's why. That's why. He's cool, like, you know, he'll mind his business, but like lately this task force, they raided the Rainbow Lounge. They made most of 'em come out to their cars. Take 'em, make 'em go through their cars, and check their cars, too."

"They check their cars?"

"Yeah. That's about the third or fourth time they got that place. So I guess they—what they're doin' is, you know, they're gettin' hipper, they're sayin', 'Well, I mean, we go in the bar, nobody got nothin'. They have it in their car, let's check their cars, too.' So that's what they've been doin', but they just be rollin' everywhere."

"Right," Billy said, slowly testing the waters.

Mariano jumped in. "Look, they're doin' for the people who make . . . sell like twenty-five-dollar rocks. They're putting pressure on them. That fuckin' Mayor Bucci and shit."

Billy concurred, "Heated up."

Mariano was fully relaxed now—absolutely open. "There are a couple of cool cops that are on that task force, and the rest, a lot of them, like say half of them, don't like us."

Which cops were on the take? Billy wondered. He needed to know. "Right."

"But a lot of them get along with us and shit. It's good, too, 'cause you can make that businessman clientele."

"'Cause everybody wants it now 'cause it's Memorial Day," Billy said. "So everybody wants this shit for tomorrow and Monday. And then the Fourth of July's comin' up, that's when they want to order, if I can get two, three pounds."

"Yeah, once you keep them clients happy, that's it. Like when I started my business, I started with two hundred dollars."

"Man, that's it."

"That's all I had. I was happy and that's when it all started. But back then you could make good money. But now . . ."

Billy tapped his fingers on his chin. "Now it's too competitive."

Mariano grimaced. "It's not competitive, it's people tryin' to get greedy, so what they do is they'll try to go over to the customers and give it dollars cheaper. Then after a while the prices start

CHASED

gettin' lower and shit. But before, I remember I was doin' it for forty-two. I used to make back twenty somethin' for myself. Now it's hard. Now you invest twenty-two and you make six."

As Mariano complained to Billy about his meager profit figure of six thousand dollars per kilogram, his Number One Family was shattering like a vase crashing to the floor. Not only had he convicted himself with his own tongue, but now his lieutenant, Miguel Rodriguez, showed up for the buy, and Billy waited for him to do likewise.

Billy said, "It's all here, but count it, man, to make sure."

Rodriguez smiled. "I'll count it at home. I trust you. How much is supposed to be here?"

Billy wanted him to handle the cash. "Forty-eight hundred. Check you out. When I call I'll just say Jelly Bean 'cause that's what everybody calls me, Jelly Bean."

Rodriguez said, "You know my beeper number, right?"

Billy nodded his head. "Yeah."

Mariano, who had been standing back a bit, stepped forward now. "Alright."

The body transmitter recorded every word, video surveillance captured the buy. Mariano was dead, he just didn't know it yet.

Swimming in confidence, Billy felt high. This was the ultimate. He met the surveillance team in the parking lot at the Knights of Columbus hall on Park Avenue. He emerged from the car, tossing the drugs in the air, beaming with satisfaction, and waiting to be congratulated. "We got 'em now!" Then Paul Salute from the DEA blind-sided Billy with verbal fire.

"What the fuck is wrong with you!" he yelled.

"What are you talking about? What's your problem?"

"What the fuck are you doing! That's our fucking money you're playing around with. Where the fuck were you? Why didn't you tell somebody where you were going?"

"I told you I was going to follow Mariano and to call me if you had a problem with that."

"We didn't hear you."

"Of course not. My conversation was being transmitted to the car with Falcone and O'Leary."

What was supposed to be a dream celebration was fast turning into a nightmare. Billy ripped his badge from his wallet. He slammed it on the car.

"Fuck you!" he screamed at Salute. "I don't need this fucking job. I put my life on the line and you care more about the money than you do about my life. Something happened there that was out of my control."

It wasn't until later that Falcone and O'Leary told Billy that they had cut the radio off. The next day, Billy was at the DEA office working on paperwork when Salute came over to apologize.

"That incident was the first time that I felt expendable, even though you put your life on the line for cases not a lot of cops wanted to take," Billy says. "The only reward I got was from the job—it meant everything to me. Billy Perez used to tell me, 'I should have you committed. Some of these cases you take, you must be out of your mind.'"

Still, Billy's infiltration of the Number One Family brought relief to the city. One week later, the authorities decided on a raid of Mariano's criminal enterprise at a dozen locations in the city. It was to be a massive joint effort between local, state, and federal law enforcement officials. Even though Billy was the undercover who nailed Mariano, he was asked to participate in the raid.

"Sometimes I thought I'd get killed doing undercover work and raids, but the manpower was so bad that I did everything. Undercover cops run a risk doing raids, because drug dealers have an opportunity to see you in police regalia and remember that. So I started wearing masks on them. Billy Perez and Ralphy Villegas had spent years trying to nail Mariano, so it was appropriate that they raid his house. We set it up for 6:00 A.M. Drug dealers sleep

CHASED

during the morning; they're very nocturnal. We were split up into groups; it was well organized."

Light was just breaking when police swarmed over Mariano's house that morning and shocked the leader of the Number One Family out of sleep. The search produced more than $29,000 in cash, a loaded Colt Mark IV semi-automatic pistol, a black silk "No. 1 Family" jacket with "The Boss" embroidered on the front, a drug scale, a ledger itemizing Mariano's drug payroll, and a telephone memo board with numerous telephone numbers, including the Drug Enforcement Administration number.

As the police hauled Mariano away in cuffs, his neighbors—who had been irritated by the constant flow of shady characters on their once quiet street—hissed and whistled.

On August 12, based on Billy's undercover work, a federal grand jury returned a multiple-count indictment against Mariano and twelve members of his gang for knowingly and intentionally distributing cocaine, and building a sophisticated drug organization that moved large quantities of cocaine. Mariano, who was held without bond, wrote the following unintentionally witty letter to Chief U.S. District Court Judge T. F. Gilroy Daly:

> My name is Mariano Sanchez. I am writing this letter in regards to my Federal Detainer. As you know sir, I am being held without bond at Bridgeport Community Correctional Center. This I feel is unfair. The reason I'm being held here without bond is because of the other alleged Drug Dealers that jumped bail and left the country.
>
> What I am asking, your Honor, is, I am a person who faces my troubles as a man. What others did is not my concern. I have lived in Bridgeport all my life and I have all of my family here. I am willing to do any and all time I get. I know the charges against me are serious, but in the same vein of thought, why should someone with a murder charge

get a lesser bond then me [sic]. I am not charged with any murder.

Your Honor, I am asking you for a fair and reasonable bond as is stated in the Eighth Amendment. What I am asking for is the court to be fair and if they are going to keep holding me, to bring out the facts and not rumors and come with a fair decision concerning this detainer. I would appreciate if you could reply to this letter.

Mariano asked the government to bring out the facts. Assistant U.S. Attorney Dennis King accommodated him in a response to the federal court.

"Your Honor, if this case goes to trial, the Government would show that Mr. Sanchez lived in the City of Bridgeport and ultimately, through his entrepreneurial abilities, amassed an organization that was both sophisticated and successful in moving large quantities of cocaine in the city.

"Specifically, your Honor, the Government would call Officer William Chase, who would testify that on the 27th of March, 1987, he was driving down the street in Bridgeport and saw Mr. Sanchez, who was driving a red Mazda RX7, Connecticut registration 810EOX. He recognized Mr. Sanchez from a previous surveillance. And Officer Chase put his finger alongside his nose, which is a signal used on the street indicating one's desire to obtain some cocaine.

"Mr. Sanchez indicated or gestured to Officer Chase to pull over to the side of the road, which Officer Chase did. They had a conversation wherein Officer Chase told Mr. Sanchez that he wanted some cocaine. Mr. Sanchez gave Officer Chase a telephone number and told him to call later to make arrangements to purchase cocaine.

"The Government would introduce records of the Southern New England Telephone Company which would indicate that on

CHASED

that date that telephone number, which is a mobile cellular telephone number, was subscribed to by Mariano Sanchez, Jr., 139 Seiver Circle, Bridgeport, Connecticut.

"The initial meeting between Officer Chase and Mr. Sanchez led to a number of transactions. During much of the time period after Monday, May 15, 1987, a State Court authorized wiretap went up on Mr. Sanchez's phone. A number of transactions to which I referred in preparations, negotiations for those transactions were either intercepted over the wiretap or were recorded by Officer Chase when he first met with codefendant Miguel Rodriguez, and at one point defendant Mariano Sanchez.

"On the 23rd of May another cocaine transaction took place. That transaction came about as follows: On the 22nd of May at approximately 10:15 P.M., Officer Chase beeped the defendant. Defendant returned his call, and Officer Chase and the defendant negotiated a six-ounce purchase of cocaine for $4,800. Officer Chase was told to call back about 8:00 P.M. the following day.

"On the 23rd approximately at 8:00 P.M., Officer Chase once again beeped the defendant. The defendant returned the call at approximately 8:10, and they agreed to meet in forty-five minutes in the Walbaum's parking lot where Chase and Miguel Rodriguez had met on the 19th. At approximately 9:15 P.M., defendant and Miguel Rodriguez arrived at the Waldbaum's parking lot in Bridgeport. Mr. Sanchez was in the passenger's seat of the Datsun driven by Mr. Rodriguez. At that time Officer Chase was wearing a body transmitter which allowed surveillance officers to record a conversation. Mr. Sanchez instructed Officer Chase to follow the Datsun, which Officer Chase did, and ultimately the Datsun pulled over on Maplewood Street in Bridgeport. Mr. Sanchez got out, got into Officer Chase's undercover car. Mr. Rodriguez drove away for a short time. While Rodriguez was gone Officer Chase and the defendant engaged in conversation while they waited in Officer Chase's car.

"After a time Mr. Rodriguez returned. Mariano Sanchez got out of the car. Mr. Rodriguez got in and handed Officer Chase six ounces of cocaine in return for $4,800.

"The Government would call Dr. John Zelinski of the Drug Enforcement Agency Lab who would testify that the substance was cocaine, 82 percent pure with a net weight of 169.3 grams.

"There were numerous other conversations intercepted over the wiretap on Mr. Sanchez's phone that indicated that he was the leader of the large, sophisticated drug trafficking network in Bridgeport. It became clear that it was the defendant who gave the orders in the 'Number One Family.'"

Billy's damaging evidence forced Mariano to plead guilty. He was sentenced to eighteen years in a maximum-security federal penitentiary in Texas.

Roger Falcone says, "If it wasn't for Billy, Mariano wouldn't be in jail. Billy had balls of iron. He was smart and quick, and his grasp for the job was incredible. He grabbed Mariano off balance. Billy was on duty twenty-four hours a day. You have to have nerve when you do the kind of undercover work he did. Undercover work is demanding and dangerous, and you lose that policeman's halo when you do it. Billy would take risks, sometimes to a fault, that would place him in dangerous situations."

Richard Meehan Jr., Mariano's lawyer, agrees: "Mariano had insulated himself substantially, he had been unreachable, but he let his guard down with Chase. Some people get to a point where they think they can operate with impunity. It was a complete fluke. Two or three years earlier Chase could not have gotten close to him. A ton of money was expended on an intentional basis by police, and here you end up with Chase accomplishing everything all of the other law enforcement efforts couldn't."

CHAPTER 11

Cats and Rats

THE CATS, THE RATS, the Terminators.

The Number One Family wasn't the only drug gang spreading fear and terror in Bridgeport. With Mariano Sanchez and most of his army safely tucked away, Billy was poised to set traps for other drug gangs.

Jamaicans had two drug groups, the Cats Posse and the Rats Posse. The Posses were ranked by social stature: the Cats were the elite of the Jamaicans and the Rats were the lower class. As the two groups struggled for power, violence and execution-style murders soared.

Federal, state, and local cops were frustrated time and again in their effort to infiltrate Jamaican gangs. The Jamaican culture was little understood: it was a tight-lipped, insular, deal-with-your-own mania. The feds had Sicilian-speaking agents who could infiltrate the Mafia, Spanish-speaking officers who could reach Latin gangs, and black undercovers who could mesh with black crime groups. Developing agents with a Jamaican touch—the distinctive high-boned facial features, the dreadlock hair styles, and the patois—was difficult.

The best weapons the feds had to pry information was wielding immigration laws and harassing Jamaicans with threats of deportation. Even then, shaking trees in bars frequented by Jamaicans generally proved fruitless, for a very good reason: So violent was this drug culture, if anyone snitched or was remotely suspected of it, they knew they or their family in Jamaica would be killed. Jamaicans feared their enemies more than the cops.

One was Junior Stevens, a key member of the Cats who was being vigorously pursued by Billy Chase and John Ramik, Billy's partner in the Statewide Narcotics Task Force.

"We were on this guy like white on rice," Billy says. The next day Stevens was found dead on the Lower East Side. He was found in a kneeling position, shot twice in the head, his pants pulled down to his ankles and his shoe strings tying his hands and feet behind his back.

No matter how many bars and social clubs Billy entered, no one would talk. Billy decided to turn up the heat on Jed Perkins, a known Jamaican drug trafficker.

Late one night, Billy waited for him to show up on High Street—Jed's usual beat. As soon as he spotted the citrine-skinned drug dealer, Billy came out of the shadows and grabbed him. "What do you know about Junior Stevens?"

"I don't know nothin', mon."

"Listen, if you don't come forward with something, we're going to deport your ass out of here. Tell me what you know."

"No, mon, I'm tellin you, I don't know nothin'."

"We could fuck up your life forever."

CHASED

"Mon, I don't know nothin'."

"Yeah, right," Billy began strip-searching the dealer, looking for drugs. First Billy peeled off a gray sweatshirt and jeans. Underneath was a blue warm-up suit. Beneath the warm-up suit were beige silk pants and a sweater. Inside the silk pants were designer jeans and a t-shirt. Underneath the jeans, another layer of silks. The guy could change faster than Clark Kent. Billy couldn't help laughing.

"Are you going to stop coming out of your clothes, or what?" Billy asked in amazement.

Jed shook his head vehemently. "Mon, you know, it's cold out there."

"In the middle of fucking July?"

This was a classic trick of the Jamaican gang: When things get hot and the cops are in pursuit, peel off your clothes a layer at a time and blend into a new identity.

"Shit," Billy told the guy, "you went from 180 pounds to 100 pounds in two minutes."

Jed shook his head again. "No mon, no way."

Jamaican drug dealers were so tight-lipped they wouldn't even admit to the obvious. During a raid in which Billy participated on a Jamaican club on Stratford Avenue, statewide officials brought along their drug-sniffing German Shepherd, trained to tear up drugs when he smelled them.

It was one dog of which Billy had no fear. The dog took a bite out of people only when he smelled drugs on them.

Jocylyn Crumby, the tall, slick, black-suited target of this raid, made the mistake of storing marijuana in his back pocket. While the dog could not skunk out drugs anywhere else in the club, his nose took an immediate liking to Crumby's backside. The dog lunged at him, taking a bite out of his rump.

"What the fuck is this!" Crumby shrieked, drawing back in horror as Billy and his raiding party broke up in laughter.

113

"Jocylyn, come on over here," Billy said, trying to regain his composure. "What do you have back there? Empty your pockets."

Slowly Crumby pulled the weed from his back pocket, along with his wallet. "Where did this come from?" Billy asked, holding up the bag of marijuana.

Crumby ran his finger over his gelled hair, patting it. "Mon, I don't know nothin' 'bout that."

"You don't know nothin' about that?"

"No, mon."

Billy looked at Crumby's license. "Well, whose name is on this license?"

Crumby grinned, "That's me, mon."

"Well, whose credit card is this?"

Crumby's aristocratic nose went up in the air, "That's mine, mon."

"Well, whose weed is this?"

"I don't know, mon," Crumby stared straight at Billy.

Billy laughed in exasperation. "Jocylyn, we are going to try this again. Whose credit card?"

"Mine, mon."

"Whose license?"

"Mine, mon."

"Whose herb?"

Crumby enunciated each syllable in his distinctive accent: "I don't know, mon."

"How did this shit get in here?"

"I don't know."

"Maybe it was Casper the Friendly Ghost? Fuck it, Jocylyn, you're going to jail."

Jamaican drug gangs also used their women to do their dirty work—to rent their apartments, lease cars, stash drugs, and buy guns for them. "When you'd talk to a woman who was in love with a Jamaican dealer, it was like the Jamaicans put voodoo dust on

CHASED

them. The women wouldn't talk," Billy says.

Not intentionally, anyway. Billy had ways to penetrate the tightest organizations when other cops couldn't, even though he was not Jamaican and did not look like one.

High on his list of major Jamaican traffickers was posse member Paul Anderson. Billy managed to turn an Anderson neighbor into an informant who relayed information of his operation overheard through the thin walls of Anderson's Bridgeport apartment. Informed of Anderson's comings and goings, one afternoon Billy followed Anderson from his apartment to New Haven, where the dealer exited his car and exchanged a bag of marijuana for a bag of cash. Billy arrested Anderson for the drug buy on the spot, which led Billy back to Anderson's apartment, with a probable cause search warrant signed by a judge.

During the search on Anderson's home, the phone rang. Curious, Billy picked up the receiver. On the other end was a husky-voiced woman.

"Hello?" Billy said.

"Is Paul there?"

"No, he's not here," Billy responded in his best Jamaican accent. "Who's this?"

"This is his girlfriend, Sara."

"Oh, Sara. No, he went to the store."

"Does he want me to bring anything?"

"Oh, yeah, he left a message for you to bring somethin'."

Minutes later, Sara Tyghter pulled up in front of Anderson's apartment in an indigo blue BMW. Billy walked outside to greet her.

"Hey, Sara, how are you?"

"Where's Paul? Who are you?"

"Paul's not here, but the police are. Let's see what goodies you have in the trunk of your car."

Billy opened the trunk. Inside were a mountain of drugs—ten

pounds of cocaine, ten pounds of marijuana, and $80,000 in cash. A check of Anderson's safety deposit box in his bank revealed another $180,000. The search warrant wiped him out financially. Anderson's girlfriend received five years in prison. As for Anderson, he had other ideas. Convicted of big-time drug trafficking and facing twenty years, Anderson decided to boycott the sentencing. He fled.

Billy did not come in contact with Paul Anderson again—not directly. However, shortly after Billy retired briefly to Atlanta, he was sitting in his motel room and picked up the *Atlanta Constitution,* scanning the front page. There he found a story about Atlanta's Most Wanted list featuring none other than Paul Anderson, who was wanted in Atlanta for Billy's arrest warrant. Billy's stay in Atlanta was short. "Sometimes, it was like I couldn't get far enough away from these people," Billy says.

☐   ☐   ☐

Another Cats member high on Billy's list was Joe B. Hall, a big-time cocaine and weed dealer who lived in Bridgeport's North End. Hall made it a habit of bouncing around and putting nothing in his name that would lead to his current address. Convincing neighbors to provide information on a local drug dealer who happens to live next door is never an easy thing. Although no one except a drug buyer wants a drug dealer on their street, the thought of a retaliatory strike by a violent criminal often stifles the will.

The only information Billy had was a picture of Hall and a tip relating the general vicinity where he lived. Cruising along McKinley Avenue, Billy spotted a girl about eight years old climbing the steps to her house. Watching her idly for a moment sparked an idea in Billy. He pulled over to the curb, exited his car, climbed the steps, and knocked on the door. A thirtyish man with a bald spot answered. The little girl stood next to him. Billy flashed his badge and pulled out the picture of Joey B. Hall.

Billy waved the picture. "Hi, I'm a police officer. We're looking for this person. Have you seen him?"

"I'm not sure," the man shrugged his shoulders. Billy glanced at the young girl and then looked back at her father.

Lowering his tone, Billy continued. "We're looking for him because this guy molests little children."

"What!" The man pulled his little girl closer to him.

Billy met his eyes. "Yeah, he molested a little girl. How old is your daughter, about eight? As a matter of fact the girl he molested was eight."

"You're kidding me."

"I'm not."

"Let me see that picture again."

Billy showed him the picture.

"That motherfucker lives right over there."

The protective father pointed to Hall's house. He told Billy the kind of car Hall drove and the general times he would come and go. As far as Billy knew, Hall was no child molester, but the information led to a raid. A search warrant executed on Hall's house picked up an assortment of narcotics. They put the drug dealer behind bars for five years.

Of course, Billy felt good about the outcome, but it didn't obscure his feeling that every time he caught one drug dealer, two more seemed to spring up in his place. One of these, Frankie Estrada, was the head of the Terminators, a drug gang that fashioned its name from the fate of people who did not pay for the dope they bought—terminated. Frankie Estrada was a fugitive on the FBI's Most Wanted list.

The first time Billy ran into Frankie Estrada, he noticed a bracelet on his wrist with the letter *F* arranged in diamonds. It was one of those details Billy filed away in his computer-like brain.

One night Billy was driving home after an evening of raids when his stomach began growling. He was a McDonald's freak. A couple of Big Macs, extra large fries, a coke, a piece of apple pie—just the things to satisfy a stomach after a hard evening of work. He stopped into McDonald's on I-95 in Fairfield, Connecticut, one of the busiest franchises in the McDonald's chain. Standing at the counter to place his order, Billy eyed a burly, brown-haired man standing next to a wiry guy who never took his eyes off the larger man ordering a Big Mac. The burly guy looked incredibly like Estrada. Billy focused his eyes intently. He looked at the man's wrist. The bracelet was there.

"Hey, Frankie," Billy said nonchalantly.

"No, I ain't Frankie. I'm his brother."

"And I'm Jorge Colon, his friend, so I ought to know," the wiry guy nodded.

Billy wouldn't take his eyes off the larger man. "No, man, you're fucking Frankie," Billy added, pointing his finger at him. "You're Frankie, man."

"No, no, I can prove it. Let me go out to the truck and get my license." The burly guy met Billy's stare.

Billy was in a precarious situation. He was staring down Frankie Estrada, a known cop-shooter, the head of the Terminators, inside a McDonald's loaded with people. In addition, Estrada had one of his gang members with him. This could get messy.

Billy knew he had to make a show of strength. His voice became steel-edged. "Okay, Frankie, let's go outside to check your identification." Colon, his eyes smoldering, followed them. As they walked outside, Billy patted Estrada around the waist, feeling for a gun. "Hey, Frankie, you're putting on a few pounds, man. You must be eating at McDonald's a lot."

"I told you, I'm not Frankie." Estrada slicked back his thick hair.

Billy pulled out his gun and shoved Estrada against the exterior wall of the eatery. Billy felt for his handcuffs. *Damn*, he had left them in his car.

CHASED

"Frankie, don't you move or I'll fucking kill you!" Billy said.

Estrada's companion began to walk away. Did he have a gun? Things could get out of control—fast.

"Stay where the fuck you are," Billy told Colon. "You guys don't mean shit to me. I just shot a motherfucker last month, and I shoot below the waist."

With patrons walking in and out of McDonald's, Estrada began to scream. The whispers of the passers-by grew louder now. "Look at that black crook."

Hearing them, Billy's heart missed a beat. How many times, because of his color, had he been mistaken for the very criminal element he was after. How many times would it happen in the future? He choked back the bitter taste rising in his mouth. Holding his knee against Estrada's back, Billy pulled out his police badge.

"I'm a police officer," Billy told them. "Please call 911 and tell them an officer needs assistance."

Instead the customers wheeled around and headed for their cars. It happened that the State Police Troop G Barracks in Westport was just minutes away. You could almost always count on a Statie to stop at McDonald's, and Billy desperately hoped one would do just that now.

"Help, he's robbing me!" Estrada continued.

Billy shouted over to Estrada's partner.

"Get the paperwork out of the truck. I want you to come back with your hands over your head."

A few minutes later, Colon showed Billy the paperwork, but no evidence to support the claim that his companion was Frankie's brother.

"Frankie, you're all through. You're going to jail tonight."

"Fuck you I am," Estrada retorted.

Meanwhile, two members of the Terminators who were staked outside of the McDonald's in their parked cars pulled rifles from their vehicles and loaded up. Billy had his back to them. They poised their weapons.

At that moment, alerted by the McDonald's manager, state troopers simultaneously zoomed into the parking lot with lights blazing and sirens roaring. Never had Billy been happier to see anyone. The guys with the guns jumped into their cars and sped off.

"They were ready to blow you away," a gas station attendant who had witnessed the scene told Billy. "The cops pulled up just in time."

After being booked and dragged off to a cell, Estrada examined his Polo shirt, shredded in the scuffle. He yelled out to Billy, who was pacing outside the cell, "Yeah, Chase, you're a big man now. You got me. They should promote you to lieutenant. But what about my shirt? Are you going to buy me a shirt!"

"No. Fuck you."

"I bet you ate my Big Mac, too."

"I'm eating it right now."

"Hey, could you go back and get me another one?"

☐   ☐   ☐

Looking for members of drug gangs often pulled Billy into the city's notorious housing projects. One, Marina Village, the city's South End housing project, was a favorite hiding place for guys on the lam.

Only a few days after catching Estrada, on one of his slow drives through Marina Village, Billy was flagged by a man in a car who had something to sell him. Pulling up, Billy studied the man. A flicker of recognition crossed his face. This was Bernard Wright, who was wanted on a drug warrant that Billy had had issued himself.

"Hey, man, need something?" Wright asked Billy.

"I got good news and bad news," Billy responded, holding up a one-hundred-dollar bill, with his police badge behind it. "The good

CHASED

news is I got a hundred bucks. The bad news is, Bernard, you're under arrest."

Bernard Wright was six-foot-six, 230 pounds—something that did not occur to Billy right away. Wright could chew up and spit out cops with a badge and an arrest warrant. As Wright opened the door to his car and unfolded his huge body, Billy shook his head.

"Damn, Bernard, you're a big motherfucker."

Billy looked up the street for back-up, hoping help was within reasonable reach. Wright wasn't just big—he was super-human. And he was always ready to fight. And in Marina Village, residents were always willing to watch him fight. It didn't take long for a crowd to gather around their cars.

Wright threw his gargantuan arms forward. Billy, a dedicated karate student who loved testing what he learned at school in the field, grabbed onto Wright's lunging arm, turned Wright over his hip, and flipped the stout man to the ground.

Billy stood over Wright, smiling as though he had the big man where he wanted him. So he thought. Wright quickly jumped to his feet and blasted Billy with a series of right hooks. As Billy fought back, trading punch for punch, his back-up from Statewide arrived. It turned into a law enforcement pile-on. Billy was on top of Wright's back, John Ramik jumped on Billy, and Terry Boone piled on, too. Wright was hauling around six hundred pounds of cops on his back like Hulk Hogan carrying wrestlers in a special handicap match.

Billy pulled out the handcuffs and grabbed Wright's arm, tugging it around his back. Then Billy stuck his forearm close to Wright's face. Wright opened his mouth and sunk his teeth deep into Billy's arm. He ripped away at Billy's flesh.

Billy screamed in agony, "You motherfucker!"

Wright was an immovable object. Short of shooting him, Billy needed an irresistible force to move him into the police cruiser. As Ramik and Boone continued the fight, Billy raced to his car, reached in, and pulled out a blackjack.

Running back to the ruckus, Billy swung the blackjack and connected with the fleshy back part of Wright's huge neck. Feeling the full impact of the immobilizing blow, Wright's body jerked forward. The cops shoved Wright into the car.

Billy discovered that in the heat of battle he had lost his wallet, credit cards, money, badge, and all of his identification. Cops don't like it when people are ripped off. They like it even less when they're ripped off. This called for a speech. To no one in particular, to everyone in general, Billy addressed the crowd.

"Look, all you guys know I'm a fair motherfucker. I don't plant shit on anybody. If I do somebody, he's done the right way. I want my shit back. I'm going to be a resident down here until I get my shit back!"

For the rest of the day and evening, Marina Village was Public Enemy Number One. Every cop Billy could pry loose from the FBI, DEA, State Police, and local PD saturated the housing project looking for Billy's wallet and badge. Anything that breathed got the treatment.

"What's your name?" "Who are you?" "Do you have any ID?" "Is your car registered?" "Where's Chase's stuff?"

Marina Village was shut down. Drug dealers couldn't make a move. For them, it was a nightmare of the worst kind. Billy went to the hospital to get treatment for the bite wound. Wright's teeth marks are a permanent memento on Billy's scraped arm. At 2:00 A.M. the phone rang at police headquarters. "Send a car down to Marina Village, Apartment 3-A. We have Chase's badge."

A patrol car was sent out. When the patrolman knocked on the door, there was no answer. As the cop waited, a bag containing Billy's badge was quietly placed on the back of the patrol car. The cop did not see the bag on the back of the cruiser and drove off when no one responded at the door. The bag fell off the car and into the road. The cops received another call.

CHASED

"Send the cop back! The badge was on the car and he didn't see it. We got the shit."

Later that morning Billy went to Marina.

"Billy, they had your shit last night," an informant told him. "They put it on the cop's car but he didn't see it. So they put the stuff in the dumpster over by Building 21."

"The fucking dumpster?" Billy asked in disbelief. He walked to the metal trash bin, swung the cover over to the side, and looked inside. The dumpster was loaded with trash. Billy called the maintenance man at Marina for help.

They pulled out all of the garbage. At the bottom of the dumpster, inside a paper bag, inside a plastic bag, inside a rag was Billy's badge, identification, wallet, money, credit cards—everything.

Feeling triumphant, Billy left holding his belongings above his head like the victory celebrant raising the tennis cup at Wimbledon. A group of Marina residents cheered his departure.

CHAPTER 12

Sorry, Ma

WITH HIS WALLET, money, and badge returned, Billy got back to the business of seeking out drug kingpins. He set his sights on Carlos Agosto, an East Side drug dealer.

Forty-eight hours later, Billy set up a half-pound buy in the parking lot of the Burger King on the East Side.

Leaning against his car, looking around for surveillance coverage, Billy met with Agosto associate Danny Acosta.

"Hey, give me the money," Acosta told Billy.

"You crazy? Get the product," Billy replied.

"Look," Acosta responded, "if I wanted to kill you right now I could."

Under normal circumstances, such a threat posed no real significance to Billy. Idle threats, verbal posturing, sizing up your customer were fairly routine in drug buys. But some guys are just crazier than others. As Acosta spoke, he stuck a .357 Magnum underneath Billy's chin. Billy clenched his fists. This was serious.

"I could fucking kill you and take the money right now!"

"Oh, shit, I can see that," Billy reasoned.

Then Acosta surprised Billy again—he smiled. "But I won't kill you. Here, take the gun."

Acosta held out the gun. Shook up, Billy grabbed onto it.

"Do you trust me now?" Acosta asked.

As Billy nodded in the affirmative, Agosto reached down and rolled up one leg of his pants to his thigh. In plain view bulged a half-pound bag of cocaine.

Billy swallowed hard. "I'll go get the money," he said. At that point Billy's surveillance team merged on the scene.

Agosto sprinted into the Burger King. The feds followed with their guns raised, horrifying the lunchtime crowd. Patrons ducked under tables, hit the floor, and jumped over the fast-food counter, hiding behind it. Meanwhile, the feds grabbed Agosto and threw him down spread-eagle on the floor. Billy too was hammered to the floor. Billy threw in a little play acting to keep up his sting cover.

"You set me up; I'm going to fuck you up," he screamed at Agosto and Acosta.

The officers pulled Billy away in handcuffs and tossed him in the back seat of the police cruiser. Next came Agosto and Acosta.

"I knew you were a fucking snitch," Billy swore at them.

"I ain't no snitch. What's your problem," Acosta said.

Later that day, with the drug sellers booked and another day winding down, Billy picked up the phone to check in with his mother. When she heard his voice, she burst into tears.

"I can't believe you could do this to me, to our family," she cried.

"Ma, what are you talking about?" Billy asked, confused.

Her voice rose dramatically. "Change your name. I don't know

CHASED

how you could disgrace us like that."

"Like what, ma, like what?"

His mother poured out the story between sobs. One of her former co-workers at St. Vincent's Medical Center had been in Burger King during the time of the arrests. The woman saw Billy lying on the floor, being arrested and hauled away. She called his mother to tell her what she witnessed.

For Nellie Chase, the news was shocking. Billy—not wanting his mother, living in retirement in another state, to worry about the dangers of his undercover work—had not told Nellie Chase he was a specialized undercover for the Bridgeport Police Department. She thought he was still a Monroe cop, chasing dogs and cows.

"Ma, I wasn't arrested for real," Billy explained. "It's part of my job. Ma, you worry too much, and I didn't want to tell you. I work undercover for Bridgeport. The arrest was part of a sting operation."

"A sting operation?" his mother repeated, astonished. "You're not in Monroe?"

"No, ma," Billy slowly explained it all again. "I'm in Bridgeport. I work with the feds and state on drug cases."

For a moment there was complete silence. Then Nellie Chase sighed heavily. "That's a relief. When you called, I thought you were calling from jail."

"I am, ma," he laughed.

Billy was glad to put his mother's immediate fears to rest, but he wondered what she would think of his other subterfuges, especially the one in which he played garbage man.

You can learn a lot about people from their garbage—the kind of food they eat, the liquor they drink, the clothes they wear. And, of course, the drugs they sell and consume.

An old shoe, runny panty hose, moldy bread, sour milk, greasy sauces smearing week-old meats, maggot-infested fish. Could domestic trash really become someone else's treasure? Only if you're an undercover like Billy Chase, who'd be up to his elbows in garbage to put a drug dealer in jail. For Billy, sifting through a bag of trash was like digging deep into the bottom of a Cracker Jack box. So maybe the peanuts were too old to eat, but what a surprise when you're all done. In some cases, the surprise was a trace of drugs, a search warrant for a house, and a huge drug raid.

When Billy had difficulty getting inside a drug dealer's operation, he and John Ramik would put on their garbage clothes, stake out a dealer's house, and wait for the trash to be placed curbside for searches in the middle of the night. It all seemed so logical to Billy. After all, he reasoned, once people put their garbage curbside, they were disowning it, weren't they? Why would it matter if someone took a peek?

Billy and Ramik would argue over whose car would carry the stinking garbage bags over to the spacious parking lot at Central High School where they sorted through the stuff sprawled out on the pavement. "Hey John, let's take your car today. My car still smells like shit from the last garbage haul," Billy said. The haul was never pretty, nor pleasantly aromatic, but the payoff was big. Ramik in particular loved the challenge of inspecting someone else's leftovers.

"John, you really like this shit, don't you," Billy said to his partner, shaking his head.

John shrugged. "Yeah, you're really funny. But seriously, think how much we're learning about this guy. Look at this. I never knew his wife wore such cheap perfume."

"That's nothing. Get a load of her old man's underwear. Look at the size of these mothers."

John held up a mashed-up tube that looked like squashed toothpaste. "Billy, you need some K-Y Jelly?"

Billy laughed. "No thanks. Keep it for yourself."

Anytime they found plastic bags with traces of powder, they confiscated them. They could be tested at the police lab. If the stuff

CHASED

tested positive Billy and Ramik typed up search warrants and paid a visit to the occupant of the house from which they confiscated the garbage. These raids produced big drug stashes, scales, needles, and a variety of other drug paraphernalia.

Billy's garbage forays even landed him a fugitive, two thousand miles away on the lam in Las Vegas. Stennett Chapman, who was featured on the "America's Most Wanted" television series, was wanted for two murders in connection with a Jamaican narcotics operation in New York. A federal SWAT team thought his girlfriend in Bridgeport might know his whereabouts. Billy staked out her apartment.

Rather than bolt through the front door with guns blazing, Billy play-acted his "maintenance man" routine. Billy knocked on the door. A woman answered.

"Excuse me, ma'am," Billy smiled humbly, "a bunch of tenants complained to me about their heat not working. I just want to check out a few things to make sure your heat is okay."

"It's warm in here. Do you have to do this now?" the woman responded. "It's early."

"Hey, lady, I know it's early. I don't want to be here either, but you got kids in here. You want them to freeze later?"

"Okay, come in." She opened the door.

Billy moved in quietly and quickly without disrupting the sleeping children. The SWAT team followed. They looked around. No boyfriend.

"Okay, where can we find him?" asked John Serano, a special agent with the FBI.

"I don't know, I haven't seen him in a while."

"Look, this guy bailed out on you. He's no good to you anymore, so let us know where he might be."

"I don't know. He likes to go to Las Vegas, maybe he's in Vegas."

"Where in Vegas?"

"I don't know if he's in Vegas. He could be anywhere."

Billy looked at the woman's garbage can in the kitchen. It was brimming over with garbage.

"Hey, we're sorry we had to do this to you," Billy told her. "I know you must be under a lot of stress—you have children to take care of, a house to maintain. Things aren't easy. You don't even have a man around to take your garbage out."

"Yeah," she said, "tell me about it."

"Listen, that bag of garbage looks heavy. We're on our way out, so I'll take it out for you."

What woman would ever turn down a man's invitation to take out the garbage? Back in the car, Billy held up the bag of garbage.

"Chase, what are you doing with that garbage?" asked Serano.

"Oh, relax, the lady said I could take it."

"We can't."

"Look, she said it was garbage, I could have it, so I took it. It's garbage. That's all."

Billy began sifting through the smelly mess. Halfway through the bag, Billy pulled out the woman's phone bill.

"Hey, John, here's a gold mine—a couple of numbers in Vegas. Let's have the Feds check them out."

The phone numbers led the feds to the Tropicana Hotel in Las Vegas where, sure enough, Chapman was staying. The FBI apprehended the fugitive—all because Billy burrowed into his girlfriend's trash.

Eventually newspaper articles chronicled Billy's garbage-gathering investigations, and drug dealers became hip to the technique. Throughout the drug trade there was an awful lot of talk about garbage. "Don't put it out in the street," the word went up. "Find other ways to get rid of it."

"After that some of the drug dealers used to keep garbage in their house weeks at a time because they didn't know what to do with it," Billy says, grinning. "At least we got to stink up their

CHASED

homes instead of vice versa."

Despite his good humor, jokes, and growing reputation, Billy knew his mother would not have liked his playing with garbage. That was for sure after what she had sacrificed to send him through school, and he knew she would have liked even less the drinking and carousing at notorious bars that sometimes went with his job.

El San Juan Cafe in Norwalk, Connecticut, was a Colombian bar. No Puerto Ricans, no Dominicans, no blacks, no Anglos. They didn't have to place a "Colombians Only" sign in the door—everyone knew it. Like the Jamaicans, Colombians were insular. They dealt only with themselves. They spooked easily. You did not go into the bar unless you were Colombian. Or unless you were Billy Chase.

"Shit, I'll make friends with these guys," Billy told his friends in Statewide. "I'll go into the bar and we'll party."

"Forget it, Billy," he was told. "You're black and you're not Colombian. They'll never let you in."

Telling Billy Chase that something was impossible was all the incentive he needed. One night a few weeks later, Billy walked into the Colombian cafe, all smiles, full of life, as though he was everyone's best friend ready to lead them to the mountain top. Colombians were everywhere, drinking at the bar, shooting pool, watching television, bantering at the tables.

Olive-complected men in white suits looked up from their drinks, more annoyed than angry that a black man with a gregarious patina would dare enter their bar. They surveyed him. He was smiling. He was cracking jokes. And he was alone. He was probably too stupid to realize that he had entered a Colombian bar. The verdict: he was harmless. They would concentrate on drinking.

Billy needed to make a friend, so he sat next to Alejendro Montoya and ordered a rum and coke.

"Hey, how ya doing?" Billy introduced himself. "I'm Malik. So what's up?"

Montoya was unimpressed and remained silent.

"Yeah, man, I hear this is the place to be, the place to hook up," Billy continued. "Can you hook me up?"

"I don't know what you're talking about," Montoya stared at the interloper.

Billy shrugged. "All I want to do is buy an ounce. What's up?"

"I don't know what you're talking about," Montoya repeated, his voice a monotone.

"Alright, let me at least buy you a drink. What do you have there, a rum and coke? Can you handle a double?"

"Yeah, I can handle it."

Billy ordered two drinks. The bartender set one in front of each man. Billy downed his drink in a gulp, a fast blast, as though he had a train to catch. He turned to the man next to him. "I drink mine fast. Your drink is still there. Can you handle another one?"

"Yeah, I can."

Billy nodded to the bartender. "Okay, two more, please."

"Okay," Montoya said grudgingly.

Billy heard the slight change in his voice. "That's cool. Now, why do you have to act all fucking ill to me? I come in here to buy a few drinks, make conversation. I'm in here all the time. I wouldn't even be here talking to you if I wasn't cool."

"I don't know what you're talking about." Montoya's guard was up again.

Billy sighed, "Here we go again." He signaled the bartender, "Hey, give me two more drinks."

Eight drinks were on the table, four for Billy and four in front of Montoya. Now it was show time. Fast and furious, Billy downed the drinks one by one. *Gulp. Gulp. Gulp. Gulp.* He looked over to Montoya. He had invoked the macho drink thing, and Montoya had to keep pace. He downed all four in rapid-fire succession. Without saying it, it was his way of saying, "I can keep up with you."

"I know you must be feeling this shit, eh," Billy said with a

CHASED

wave of his hand indicating the empty glasses.

"No, I ain't feeling shit. You Americans don't know how to hold your shit."

Billy smiled, "Yo, bartender, two more doubles. Look, I don't want to stay here drinking with you all night. Can't you just hook me up with some shit?"

"I don't know what your talking about." Montoya made a sound halfway between a grunt and a cackle. He tried to play dumb, but no longer was he straight-faced. He was becoming drunk. His responses began to be accompanied by giggles, chuckles, and cackles. As the rum seeped into the bloodstream of both drinkers, the conversation loosened up.

"How about two more? Think you can handle it?"

"Yeah, I can handle it." Giggle, giggle.

"Okay, how much for an ounce?"

"Well, how much do you want?"

"How about two ounces?"

Laughing, entirely drunk, and slipping off his stool, Montoya reached into his pocket. Oblivious to the surroundings, his life but a buzz, he pulled out a bag of cocaine and plopped it on the bar.

"Here ya go, Americano."

Billy ordered more drinks. They consumed fifteen rum and cokes apiece in half an hour. Montoya, a huff and a puff away from falling on the floor, was a drunken mess. Billy was drunk but scared himself sober—at least for the moment. Billy took two ounces of cocaine from Montoya and stuck the dope in his pocket. He got up from his stool and headed toward the door. Billy looked back.

"I told you, you can't hold your fucking liquor," Billy said. "I'm getting ready to walk out of here with two ounces and I haven't even paid you for them."

"Oh, yeah, that's right," Montoya chuckled, with a wave of the hand.

"You're so fucked up you'd probably sell me your mother."

Billy paid Montoya, stumbled out of the bar, and drove back to the State Police Barracks. He would arrest Montoya another day. With fifteen rum and cokes in him, he was scheduled to lead a raid that night in Bridgeport. Billy was teamed up with trooper Julio Fernandez, who had a reputation for being cheap. It was said of Julio that he wouldn't even buy his informants a cup of coffee. As he and Billy rode in the car to Bridgeport for the evening raiding party, it was clear to Julio that the effect of all the liquor had finally taken its toll on Billy. His eyes blinked on and off. His head nodded. He passed out.

"Bill, Bill, are you okay?" Julio said, touching Billy's shoulder. Billy jerked his head up.

"Yeah, motherfucker, I'm okay. I'm just tired. Can't I sleep until we get to Bridgeport?"

"I just want to make sure you're okay."

"Yeah, I'm okay." Billy nodded off again.

Julio stopped at Dunkin Donuts. He shook Billy awake. "I'll be right back."

A few minutes later he returned carrying a large mug of coffee and three donuts. "Here, Bill, it's on me."

Billy was shocked sober. This was not the Julio Fernandez he knew.

"You're buying me donuts and coffee? Motherfucker, you won't even buy your informants coffee."

CHAPTER 13

Rich Druggies, Poor Druggies

SPRING, 1988. The imposing message on the black and white poster of a skeleton absorbed the eyes of anyone who walked into the class room of Thomas Miller. "Cocaine kills. It strips life down to the bone."

Thomas Miller was a forty-two-year-old teacher who taught a course warning teenagers about the dangers of drug abuse at Westhill High School in Stamford, Connecticut. Sporting a doctorate in psychotherapy, Miller lectured students on human behavior topics such as family relations, sex education, and substance and alcohol abuse in his Family Life classes. Known as Dr. Miller, he was respected and popular.

However, one important fact had escaped the students, faculty, and administrators at Westhill. Dr. Miller lived two lives: one of drug education teacher, another of drug dealer.

As an undercover for the Statewide Narcotics Task Force, Billy collected a number of key informants for the cases he worked in lower Fairfield County, Connecticut. Known as the Gold Coast, it featured people with some of the highest disposable incomes in America.

One informant tipped Billy off that a cocaine operation was being operated by Dr. Miller and a Raymond "Ty" Williams, a record producer in Westport, Connecticut. Together, Dr. Miller and Ty sold cocaine predominately to the gentry of wealthy Westport and its environs.

Billy checked out Ty's elegant Westport mansion: the marble pillars, the stately evergreens lining the driveway. He felt more than a bit conspicuous in this exclusive part of town. "I felt like I couldn't get next to this guy's neighborhood unless I put a butler's uniform on," Billy says.

Feeling out of place, Billy rode around Westport, the homes of Paul Newman, Christopher Walken, Phil Donahue and Marlo Thomas, recording stars Michael Bolton and Neil Sedaka, and a variety of artists, writers, publishing executives, and therapists. Westport is famous for its therapists. Just about every resident has one.

Though Ty lived in Westport, good old Dr. Miller lived in Bridgeport, Billy's backyard. With the help of the informant, Billy hooked up with Ty and Dr. Miller through a series of telephone conversations. Billy arranged for a buy. One early spring afternoon, Billy went to Miller's house, accompanied by John O'Leary of the Statewide Narcotics Task Force. As they walked up to the entrance, O'Leary turned to Billy. "Remember, the hit signal is 'Fresh Package.'" Billy nodded.

Both men were there waiting for them.

"Hey, what's up, doc?" Billy asked flippantly.

CHASED

The doctor rejected any pretense of humor. "How are you?" he said stiffly.

Billy wasn't about to accept such disdain from a dealer. "You ready to do some business?"

Without replying, Dr. Miller pulled out a bag containing four ounces of cocaine. It had a street value of $50,000.

"Not bad, doc," Billy said, with a nod of approval. Speaking into his body recorder, Billy gave his surveillance team the hit signal: "Man, doc, that's a fresh package, the freshest package I ever saw."

No answer. Billy's body transmitter was not being picked up by his surveillance team staked outside. He tried again.

"Boy, what a fresh package," Billy said again, into the microphone a bit louder this time. "Fresh as can be."

Dr. Miller looked at Billy oddly. It was becoming increasingly clear to Billy that the surveillance team could not hear their conversation. He shrugged. No big deal. He'd make the arrest himself.

"You know, doc, I have some bad news," Billy said, looking at the bag of cocaine.

"What's wrong, you don't like the stuff?" Dr. Miller asked.

Billy shook his head. "No, the stuff looks okay."

"So, what is it?" the doctor asked.

Billy met his eyes. "Doc, you're under arrest. And so are you, Ty," Billy added, flashing his badge and grabbing Ty, who was already moving away.

"Oh shit," Dr. Miller said quietly. "You're going to arrest me now?"

Billy nodded, "Yeah, doc, we are."

Dr. Miller sighed heavily, "I'm glad you're going to arrest me now, because I'm so sick of this shit. I told Ty I didn't want to do this anymore. This stuff was driving me crazy. Thank you so much. Please put the handcuffs on me."

Billy looked long and hard at Dr. Miller with a mixture of pity and disgust. "No problem, doc. I'm glad you're cooperating."

Ty, however, had other ideas. While Miller and Billy were talking, Billy still had a grip on Ty's jacket. Suddenly, as Ty bolted, his jacket was flapping in the wind. Billy chased after him. Ty ran outside and around the house with Billy in pursuit, leaving Miller in his house. Ralphy Villegas, who was part of the surveillance team, picked up the chase and joined in, running behind Billy, and a couple of others from Statewide were running behind Ralphy, all chasing Ty. After a couple of futile passes around the house, Billy sprinted ahead and tackled Ty by his ankles. Unfortunately the others didn't stop, and everyone toppled on Billy like fallen dominoes. When the pile sorted itself out, Ty was cuffed and tossed into a State car.

Back in the house, Dr. Miller had not moved.

"Doc, we're going to search your house, okay?" Billy said.

"Sure, go ahead."

A search of the house turned up additional cocaine, scales, and four handguns.

The next day, newspapers across Connecticut carried the headline "Teacher is Drug Dealer." Students were stunned, co-workers shocked, and school officials had to face the embarrassing news that a teacher who taught a course on the dangers of drug abuse was, in reality, a drug user and pusher. It was a public relations nightmare.

Miller received a two-and-a-half-year prison sentence, most of which was served in a supervised home-release program. He was fired by the Stamford Board of Education, and the Connecticut Board of Education revoked his teaching certificate.

Miller protested the revocation of his teaching license, claiming his classroom experience and rehabilitation could be positive tools in teaching students how to cope with life. No one was convinced.

Driving back from Dr. Miller's sentencing, Billy and John O'Leary decided to stop at a Burger King off I-91. Occupying

CHASED

several booths and standing at the counter placing food orders were a number of Jamaicans engaged in conversation.

Billy looked at O'Leary. "What is this, a drug convention? I could make a buy out of here."

"No you couldn't," O'Leary said.

"I bet you a cheeseburger I make a buy off of these guys."

"You're on."

O'Leary ordered food and took a seat.

Billy moved next to one of the Jamaicans at the counter.

"Hey, wassup?"

"Nothin'."

"You guys got a convention going on around here?"

"No."

"What, do you guys work together?"

"We work up at the apple orchard up the road."

"What do you do up there?"

"We pick apples, mon."

"Shit, they must pay you well. Man, I know you guys must have some bad fucking weed. I know you must have some good herb."

"Yeah, mon, the best, mon. It's a chief export."

"Hey, where are you from?"

"Kingston, mon."

"I got a little thing going. I may need something. Can we hook up or somethin'? Give me your name, I'll come down to Jamaica to get the shit."

"I'm going back home, and I'm flying into Miami next month, and I'll bring some shit back."

"Well, who do you work for?"

"Dole."

"I thought they sold bananas."

"They do, but they offered us jobs to come over here to pick apples."

139

"Don't you worry about customs?"

"No, we work for Dole. There's no problem with customs, mon."

Billy went over to sit with O'Leary. He showed him the name and address of the man from Jamaica.

"Okay, John, I'm ready for my cheeseburger."

Later, Billy ran a computer check on the man he met at Burger King. The name came up on a list of Jamaican smugglers. The Dole name provided drug smugglers a shield of credibility when they passed through U.S. Customs. Corporate work in the United States often immunized them from intensive customs scrutiny.

Dole wasn't the only fruit company that drew the attention of U.S. Customs. Billy worked with the federal agency on several investigations into cocaine smuggled into Bridgeport Harbor by boat workers for the Turbana Corporation. In one case, Colombian nationals hauled huge shipments of cocaine into port with bananas from Central America.

An investigation spearheaded by Billy and Gary Cole, one of his partners in Statewide, turned up a 150-pound seizure of cocaine. Four Colombian nationals were arrested and deported.

"Billy was one of the best," says Cole, who worked with Billy on a number of banana boat investigations. "He was innovative and extremely dependable, you could not beat the kind of work he did. If he hadn't been a cop, he would have been a great drug dealer."

Some of the banana boat searches frustrated Billy to no end. Staked out overnight, waiting for the ships to come in, he'd climb through port holes, up ladders, and squeeze through the tiniest storage areas in search of drugs. Many of the searches came up empty, but that never stopped Billy from trying to trip up the workers on the freighters.

In one search, Billy came face to face with Malaysian boat workers. "Any of you guys speak English?" he asked about forty of the Turbana workers gathered about as he searched through the

CHASED

ship. The hired hands looked at Billy in silence.

"What's wrong? You guys don't talk?"

Still no response.

Billy continued his search. A couple of roaches squirming about the barrels of sugar caught his eye. Since they wouldn't talk, maybe he could have a little fun with them.

"Do you guys eat sugarcoated roaches or something?"

From the crowd a voice roared. "No, we don't eat no sugarcoated roaches!"

"Hey, who said that?" Billy fired back. "Which one of you speaks English?"

Everyone clammed up. Billy was in a playful mood. He walked up to one of the workers. "You know, you're one ugly motherfucker." The man stood silent. As Billy looked away, another voice jumped out of the crowd. "Fuck you! And you're ugly, too!"

All the workers broke out into a collective laugh.

"Damn, man, I don't see one woman on this ship," Billy reminded them. "You guys come all the way from Central America without any women? You all must be fucking each other."

From the crowd again, a voice boomed, "Fuck you, you black fuck!"

"That's it!" Billy responded. "All you motherfuckers are going to jail. Stand up against the wall."

A customs agent who overheard the commotion went on deck. "What's going on here?"

"I'm arresting everybody," Billy snapped, with a wink.

"Why?"

"Because somebody in here called me a black fuck."

"Calm down, calm down, take it easy." The customs agent addressed the crowd of workers. "Okay, everyone, say you're sorry. C'mon, now."

"Okay, sorry," a couple of them mumbled.

"Okay, you're cool," Billy said. "Go back to work."

Eventually Billy learned that some of his searches came up empty because the drugs were not coming into Bridgeport. The drug hauls were being thrown overboard to smaller boats waiting on Long Island Sound and then brought into Westport.

"Westport was a huge market for drugs," Billy says. "All those millionaires living in their mansions had plenty of money to spend and boats to play in. We never knew exactly where the dealers were dropping the stuff off, just that it was somewhere in Long Island Sound. It was impossible for the Coast Guard to track. Customs does not search boats until they come into port. So these guys were—and still are—dropping this stuff off at some marker on the Sound."

CHAPTER 14

Crack Heads, Crack Fights

WITHIN LAW ENFORCEMENT circles, Billy had emerged as the undercover of undercovers. Mariano Sanchez was in jail, the Dicks brothers were behind bars, key members of the Cats Posse were put away, and the Drug Doctor had received his dose of medicine, too. Billy was at the top of his game—mature, seasoned, and getting better with each case.

"He was a workaholic," Terrance Sprankle, a special agent with the DEA, told the *Connecticut Post*. "He'd get into drug trafficking organizations that had us knocking our heads against the wall."

"He had that look about him you don't see much," added Dale Seymour, also with the DEA, who worked shoulder to shoulder with Billy on many cases. "Billy was calm, cool-headed, and at ease, whether talking to mob guys or laying some street jive on the brothers."

Federal, state, and local law enforcement officials were learning from Billy's experiences. He had a knack for deflection in the most unusual and dangerous situations. For example, paranoid drug dealers commonly ask buyers to test the stuff they're selling. Cops aren't supposed to sample drug buys, but Billy had the answers.

"I don't want to touch the package since it's closed. I went half with my boy and I don't want him to think I'm dipping on it, you know what I mean?"

Or he'd say, "I'm buying it for a girl to get some trim," the street slang for sex.

Or he'd say, "I'm on medication," or "I have a cold," or I'm this or I'm that.

If a wary seller accused him of being a cop, Billy knew how to respond: "Hey, motherfucker, you're a cop! Let me tell you something, I hate cops. Cops killed my brother. Shot him for no fucking reason."

"The idea is to make the other guy think you're a little deranged," Billy says. "It takes the heat off."

For Billy, there were emotional highs in putting away gang members no one else could come close to in the violent drug jungles of the inner city: the crack heads, the dopers, the junkies, the dealers, the guns.

Unfortunately, there were also lows. It seemed like just another cold winter evening when Billy heard voices outside his condominium. Around midnight, two men holding shiny objects—what appeared to be screwdrivers—were trying to break into his car. Billy pulled out his gun.

"Freeze!" Billy snapped. "Put you hands over your head."

One of the robbers fled. Billy grabbed the other, Eduardo Torrez, placed his gun against Torrez's head, and pushed him up

CHASED

against the garage.

"You're not going to arrest me. You're not going to put those handcuffs on me," Torrez said.

"Oh, really," Billy said. "Watch me."

"You're pretty brave with the gun in your hand. Why not make this an even fight?"

"You want an even fight? Okay, we're gonna fight."

For Billy, the challenging task of undercover work was intriguing and overwhelming. Hearing about the dangers of tracking crazed killers and drug kings makes most sane people flinch. The daily terror of facing violent men would make any normal undercover an emotional wreck. As undercovers go, Billy was well adjusted, even-tempered, and friendly, but the pressure and tension sometimes ate away at him. The fights, in a bizarre sense, were a way to vent the stress build-up. The adrenaline flow took the edge off. For Billy, a fair fight was indeed a fair fight, even if it did go against his better judgment. Torrez was just a punk trying to break into his car. This was easy. Billy stuck his gun in his pants.

Billy turned the man around. "Okay, let's go."

Billy grabbed Torrez by his arms and pulled him forward. As Torrez's body jerked ahead, Billy thrust his knee full force into the man's groin like a piston through an engine—one of those groin shots, so hard, so agonizing, that Torrez's father should have felt the impact. If Billy wanted to end a fight quickly, a knee to the groin was an accommodating weapon.

It was a move taught to him by one of the best, master karate instructor Matty Melisi, the trainer of sports figures, movie celebrities, and law enforcement officials. If you wanted to learn how to defend yourself and hurt the person trying to hurt you, Melisi was the guy to learn from. He taught his students how to knee and punch through their adversaries.

This time, however, Torrez took the knee as though it was a slap in the face. Startled, Billy stepped back. Torrez blasted a right across Billy's jaw. Billy responded with his own shot to the head. He followed the punch with another knee to the groin. Still the man fought back. Billy put together a series of rights to the man's head; each time, Torrez's head reeled back and ricocheted off the concrete wall. Billy heard the thud of head hitting concrete. He hit the man so hard he felt his right hand crack.

Billy looked down. The snow at his feet was covered with blood from both men. This was not the kind of lesson he had planned for Torrez.

"What's up with you!" Billy shouted at Torrez. "No man can take this punishment. You're going down or out."

Torrez momentarily sprang free from Billy, who tackled him to the ground. They rolled along the sidewalk through the snow, slush, and blood. Billy managed to pull one of Torrez's arms around his back. He cuffed his adversary's wrist, pulled the other arm around, and completed both wrists. Limping, he brought the thief to booking.

Examining his broken hand at police headquarters, Billy complained to his friend, Officer Ron Bailey, about the battle. "I can't believe this," Billy said to Bailey. "I must be losing it. This guy took punches that would bring walls down."

A medical analysis revealed that Torrez was supercharged on crack. Crack gave one man the strength of three, and made many users oblivious to pain.

"Fights with crack heads were unforgettable," Billy says.

There would be more fights and more injuries.

Shortly after, the DEA engaged Billy in a major narcotics investigation against Carlos Pereira, who informants said was pulling down at least $10,000 a day. Pereira moved in as Mariano Sanchez was moved out. After a series of small buys with Pereira, Billy arranged a one-pound cocaine buy in the parking lot of the Days Hotel in Bridgeport for a quick setup and final takedown.

In the parking lot, Pereira led Billy and John Ramik to a

CHASED

dumpster. "I got the whole thing . . . just the pound . . . you give me nine for that, okay?" Pereira said to Billy. Ramik showed Pereira the money.

"Where's the shit?" Billy asked. Pereira pointed to the dumpster. He reached in and pulled out a plastic bag containing cocaine.

Billy announced the hit signal to his surveillance team: "Hey Carlos, that's a fresh package." DEA Special Agent Terrance Sprankle and State Police Sergeant John Petrowski drove up to Pereira, guns drawn.

"Freeze!" Sprankle shouted. "You're under arrest." Pereira had better things to do than give up. He sprinted off. On foot, Billy and the agents chased him across Lafayette Boulevard, up the concrete steps along a Sears department store.

They split their details to gain advantage of Pereira. Pereira raced into the Sears building and pulled out a gun. Sprankle and Petrowski were on his tail, saw the gun pointed at them, and pulled back. Pereira raced outside.

Just then, Billy rounded a corner along a retainer wall overlooking Lafayette Boulevard. He came to an abrupt halt. Pereira was waiting, about ten feet away, aiming a .380-caliber Sig Sauer handgun at Billy's chest.

"Hold it, cop," Pereira told Billy. Billy's gun, from the run, had dropped into his crotch. If he reached for it, Pereira could blow a hole through his heart. There was no time to think. He had three choices: stay and be killed, stay and be taken prisoner, or run and hope for the best. He settled on the third option. In one quick desperate motion, Billy soared headlong above the wall overlooking Lafayette Boulevard. On the other side was a ten foot drop. As he tumbled down, Billy's shoulder hit the ground first, then his head, then the rest of him. He crashed down on the concrete sidewalk and rolled out into the street.

He collapsed there, his shoulder wrenched, his back pounding with pain. At that moment, Pereira was not even in his mind. His eyes and ears focused on a car parked on the sidewalk. Inside the car a child was screaming from the pain of blows struck by a frustrated mother.

With blood dripping on his yellow tank top, Billy looked at the woman. The woman looked back at him. All Billy could think about was the world of violence, disorder, defiance, and abuse that surrounded him. There had to be more to life than this—jumping over walls to dodge bullets from drug dealers, children getting hammered by their parents. Life was a battlefield.

He forced himself to remember his work; his personal mission to change this world sent another jolt of adrenaline through his body. It brought Billy to his feet. He looked south down Lafayette Boulevard and saw Pereira racing toward the Pequonnock Apartments, a city housing project and an easy place to hide. Billy began running. Along the way he found the gun that Pereira had held against his chest. Pereira had apparently dropped it in his zeal to get away. Dodging cars and pedestrians, Billy raced through the entrance to the housing project and entered the main door.

He flew up a flight of stairs and saw Pereira's legs. He ran faster. Approaching the second landing, Billy stretched out and tripped up Pereira's ankles. He jumped on Pereira's back. "Don't fucking move!" he screamed. Billy pushed his gun against Pereira, cuffed him, and led him back to the other undercover agents.

Then Billy went to the hospital. He had separated his shoulder in the fall, but neither he nor the hospital staff realized it. For six months, until he reported his continuing pain to his doctor, who made a careful examination, he had a separated shoulder and did not know it. During all this time he continued to work through the pain and the injury. Billy's undercover life was like a 200-mile-per-hour race around the Indianapolis Speedway. There was no time to sit back and cruise, no time to let up or relax. He kept on working, despite the urging of friends to step on the brakes.

CHASED

A lot of cops would have applied for disability pension right then and called it quits. Billy could not. He still had too much to do. He never forgot his mission to help break the biggest drug crime syndicate of them all—the Mafia. But the injury and the daily demands of the job were wearing on him. He took a drag from his first cigarette. One butt a day turned into one pack a day. One pack became two packs.

CHAPTER 15

Workaholic

IN ORDER FOR Billy to prove to the world and himself that he was the best undercover in the business, he had to put the demands of the job first, his home life second.

When it came to work—whether he was there or not—Billy was constantly thinking bout how to catch the dealers and creating specific plans. He dreamed about getting the Mafia. Remembering the responsibility that his parents instilled in him in childhood, he set the highest goals for himself. And Billy was unafraid of heights: the higher the mountain, the better the climb. Billy never bragged about his achievements on the job; he just did them with a modest attention to detail and a gritty determination to succeed. And he gladly shared his time and his talents with anyone who sought his expertise. If anyone asked, he was there.

This led to a weakness that was constantly exploited. He just couldn't say no. He was always the first one at the office and the last to leave.

When someone said, "Hey, Billy, I need help with this case," no problem, Billy was there. When he was asked to work overtime, even though he had just finished a double shift with almost no rest, no problem, he was glad to work. When his supervisors asked him to take a case no one else could or would, no problem, they could count on Billy.

Billy specialized in accomplishment. He was on a mission to prove his talents to himself and others. "It was the job. The job was everything," he said.

What many of his co-workers didn't know was that Billy had two children: a son produced from a relationship during college and a son from his first marriage to Janette, a marriage that ended in divorce in 1983. In 1985, he walked down the aisle with a second wife, Theresa. As good as Billy's professional life was going, his home life was a totally different story.

One day, Billy was driving his youngest son, Billy, to a Little League baseball game. It was a day to spend quality time with a son who eagerly anticipated and needed his father's attention and approval. To a Little Leaguer, there's nothing like proving yourself in front of a father encouraging your every move from the stands. But a call came in on Billy's car phone. It was one of his supervisors.

"Billy, we need you to come in," the caller said. "An important case is breaking."

"Can't it wait?" Billy asked, knowing the answer.

"We need you now."

Billy sighed, "Okay, I'll be there in a few minutes."

Billy looked at his ten-year-old son. His dejected eyes told the story.

CHASED

"You can't watch me play today, Dad?" young Billy asked.

Billy shook his head miserably. He was committed to his work, but he knew he was neglecting his son. Even though little Billy was crushed, he offered his father some words of comfort. "You know, Dad, I know you feel bad. I understand."

Working all hours of the day and night did nothing to foster good relations in his second marriage. Theresa put up with his obsession for a while, until the distance between the two proved too much. "Bill, I can't live like this," she said plaintively.

Billy asked for understanding. Theresa asked for a closer relationship, a better life. They could not reach a common ground. Their relationship grew further apart.

Despite his personal problems, Billy continued to work two shifts a day. He had his own caseload but was on loan to other law enforcement offices as well. It was Fairfield County by day, New Haven County by night.

Billy was a soft touch for anyone who needed him.

"You're the only one who can write a report and do this case," he was often told. Even when he weakly protested, it did not last long. He gave in easily. Increasingly, his supervisors and peers knew what buttons to push to get him back to work, no matter what the hour.

As the pressures of the job increased and injuries wore him down mentally and physically, the deterioration of his home life increased. The intensity of the job squeezed him into a shell. He felt that no one, beyond a couple of guys on the job, could relate to his inner fears, the stress, the constant manipulation of men who would kill him if they knew who he was. When he did go home, he was exhausted. He would go to sleep and head back to work as soon as he got up. Theresa could not reach him and eventually stopped trying. Billy became reclusive. The gulf between them widened. Billy retreated even more, believing Theresa no longer cared about him.

This was never more evident than the day he suffered his injury in pursuit of Carlos Pereira.

Billy limped into the house bandaged from the cuts, dejected from the pain, and anguished from the thought of Pereira's gun cocked at his heart. He was silent. He did not tell her about the incident. Theresa prepared herself for another silent evening.

That night Theresa's girlfriend, Debbie Davis, stopped by their house for a visit. When Theresa went to the kitchen to prepare a snack, Billy poured out his pent-up feelings to Debbie about his nightmarish day.

"You poor guy," Debbie said as Theresa walked back in carrying a tray. Theresa stared at her husband.

"Why didn't you tell me what happened?" Theresa asked. "If you don't want me, just find someone else."

"I didn't think you were concerned," Billy said.

"You never talk to me. I'm used to that; I just want to know if you're okay."

Billy's loneliness, frustration, and pain exploded.

"What am I going to talk to you about?" he said. "You don't know what I'm going through. You're not there when I need you. Don't try to show concern in front of your friend."

Billy had lost faith in his marriage. After a while, seeking an escape, he fell into an affair with a friend, Mickey Roberts. Sensitive and vulnerable, Theresa began to suspect Billy had strayed. She questioned him repeatedly about where he had been and with whom.

Billy, the prolific manipulator at work, denied her accusations vehemently. However, he had forgotten that the wife of a preeminent investigator could learn something from her husband's work. While he denied everything, she kept watching.

One afternoon, Theresa followed Billy to Mickey's apartment in the North End of Bridgeport. When Billy stepped outside of the apartment building Theresa was waiting for him, boiling with anger.

CHASED

"I know where you've been," she said to Billy.

Billy wasn't ready to give in. "Where?"

"You're screwing around on me."

"What are you talking about?" he said walking away.

It wasn't the last time Theresa followed Billy to Mickey's apartment, nor the final time he'd be confronted by a furious wife.

One afternoon, Billy received a call on his beeper. It was Mickey. "Please get over here right away," she said to Billy. "It's an emergency."

Billy raced over to her apartment. When he pulled up, he felt as though a food processor was shredding his guts—Theresa and Mickey were waiting for him. "Oh, shit," he said out loud. Billy debated what to do: drive off and head for cover, or face the music. Either way, Billy thought someone was going to die, and he was the likely candidate for an execution.

Billy was an expert at slipping out of any situation, but even Houdini would have trouble with this one. By comparison, his memory of Carlos Pereira with a gun pointed at his heart didn't seem so bad. He laughed nervously at the thought and slowly got out of his car. Inside the apartment, two pairs of eyes pointed at him like daggers. Theresa didn't waste any time. She got right to the point.

"Who do you want, her or me?" she said.

Mouth open, Billy stood in shocked silence. Theresa continued. "Make a choice right now."

"You keep saying to me, 'If you don't want me, find someone else,'" Billy responded, trying to stall for time.

"Now," Theresa said.

Billy had to make a decision. If he didn't, both of them would think he was gutless.

"I want Mickey," he said quietly.

"Okay, we're through," Theresa said. "I'm gonna take you for everything." She hopped in her car, gunned the motor, and sped off so fast the tires screamed.

The bomb in Billy's personal life was ticking. Meanwhile, in his work life he prepared for the "big one," getting the Mafia, the mission he had been waiting for since that day long ago that he had seen Frank Piccolo blown away.

CHAPTER 16

Mob Ties

BILLY'S PERSONAL LIFE was falling to pieces, but his work life was soaring like a rocket. It was his salvation. The dealers he put in jail were high on drugs; Billy was high on the people he put away. The most difficult challenges provided long-lasting emotional highs. They fulfilled his purpose—to be the best undercover of his generation. And he was. But it wasn't enough. He still could not forget the sight of Piccolo's bullet-ridden body and his promise to himself that he was going to help crack open the Mafia.

Waiting for his opportunity for years, he had kept apprised of the Mafia's activities. Shortly after Piccolo's murder, Thomas "Tommy The Bull" DeBrizzi had been installed as the head of the Connecticut faction of the Gambino crime family. He held this position with a pretty good run until he suffered the fate of so many in his peculiar profession.

On December 16, 1985, the man to whom DeBrizzi reported, Paul Castellano, was blown away along with his underboss, Thomas Bilotti, in front of Sparks Steak House on a busy midtown Manhattan street. Angelo Ruggiero, the Gambino capo Billy helped to put behind bars during the Dicks case, was a key figure in the Castellano hit. Castellano had lectured his subordinates about the consequences of violating his ban on narcotics trafficking. The Gambino boss of bosses ordered Ruggiero to turn over incriminating FBI tapes recorded from a bug inside Ruggiero's home that led to his heroin arrest. Ruggiero refused. John Gotti, Ruggiero's supervisor, feared that Castellano would vent his wrath on him as well. Gotti made his move before Castellano. With Castellano out of the way, Gotti quickly emerged as the most powerful mobster in the United States. Changes were coming.

On February 5, 1988, DeBrizzi's icy, bloated, bullet-riddled 280-pound body was discovered inside the trunk of a car in the parking lot of a Trumbull, Connecticut, shopping mall. The car that held the frozen body was parked under a movie marquee featuring the film *For Keeps*. DeBrizzi had been last seen departing the Howard Johnson's in Stamford, supposedly to resolve a problem connected with illegal gambling.

Federal informants leaked word that Gotti had decided DeBrizzi was sucking up too much of the action and replaced him with a younger, modern soldier of his liking, Anthony Megale of Stamford.

Stamford was, and is, the headquarters for such corporations as Xerox, GTE, and Pitney Bowes. Why not make it the corporate headquarters for Gotti's Connecticut operation?

So DeBrizzi was out, Megale was in, and now so was Billy Chase.

CHASED

□ □ □

During one of his countless raids, Billy confiscated a cocaine handbook that outlined how drugs were distributed throughout the country, from the top distributors, to mid-level dealers, down to street-level pushers. Skimming through the book at the Statewide offices, Billy became increasingly frustrated by the massive drug trade's international tentacles. He looked searchingly at his partner Billy Perez.

"Damn, man, why do we have to settle for the middle and bottom rung when we can do the top rung?" Billy asked Perez. "We've done the Colombian gangs, we've done the Jamaicans, we've done the blacks, we've done the Dominicans and Puerto Ricans. Let's start doing the big boys. Let's do the Mafia."

Billy had learned all he could about the reputations of these men—the wide-scale ownership of politicians, cops, labor unions, and judges—and recognized the public's unquenchable thirst to learn more about their secret society. The media had made them heroes. Billy wanted to destroy that myth. He wanted to infiltrate the lives of murderous men who kissed, then gave orders to kill, gladly attending the funerals of their victims professing sorrow. Billy also knew that the Dicks brothers, Mariano Sanchez, and various members of ruthless Colombian and Jamaican gangs would gladly attend his funeral, too, if they could. But the Mafia was the greatest challenge of all.

"Billy, the Mafia?" Perez responded, looking at Billy. "What, are you nuts? You should be in Belleview."

"What do you mean?" Billy asked.

"Chase, man, look at you."

"I look at myself all the time, so what?"

"You're fucking black!"

"Oh, come on, we can do these guys," Billy pressed on. "We've done everybody else. It's time to graduate to the big leagues."

From the day he had seen Piccolo's dead body, Billy had been preparing by learning his craft. He accepted the fact that he had to crawl before he could walk, then walk before he could sprint, but once he had earned his stripes with the Number One Family, Billy was up and running. In the drug undercover world, Billy was now considered the tops in his profession. But Billy wanted more. He wanted to bust the most deadly group of them all—the Mafia—and whether an idealist or a fool, Billy felt he could do anything.

Billy's assignment to Statewide brought him into contact with some of the brightest and most seasoned law enforcement officers in the country, such as Milo Dowling and Dave Cotton, special agents with the FBI who had spent most of their careers penetrating high-powered gangsters in the New York–based La Cosa Nostra.

Everyone, even Billy on his more pragmatic days, knew that the chances of a black man infiltrating the Italian Mafia were as likely as an all-black U.S. Senate. Like the Senate, Mafia families were run by a bunch of fat white guys who were used to doing things their own way. Anything female, or any male of color, was unacceptable except as a token. His superiors felt Billy's mission was impossible, but they also felt that with Billy's intuitive understanding of human beings, quick mind, courage, and uncanny ability to pierce the underbelly of drug groups—the qualities that had won such respect among his peers—it wasn't impossible that he could make the right connections and infiltrate drug dealers on the fringes of the Mafia's organized crime network. If by some miracle his investigations led to bigger fish, that was just an added bonus.

In fact, Billy had already earned his stripes in one regard. In his investigation of the Dicks brothers, he established that the Dickses' heroin stash was in fact supplied through Gene Gotti's New York Mafia operation, a fact he shared during Gotti's drug trial.

Special Agents Dowling and Cotton, two of the FBI's most knowledgeable agents on the inner workings of the mob in Connecticut, filled Billy in on a major cocaine trafficking operation in

CHASED

lower Fairfield County that the feds had had difficulty cracking. The feds had a target list of people, which they shared with Billy.

"Give me the fucking case, I can do this shit," Billy begged them.

The case involved drug traffickers with ties to the Gambino crime family's Fairfield County connection. The feds had achieved some success in taking down underworld figures in the Gambino, Genovese, and Patriarca crime families, the three mob families with the most influence in Connecticut. But John Gotti's ascension as the most powerful organized crime figure in the country had opened up new doors and new opportunities in Connecticut's underworld.

With Gotti's blessings, Anthony Megale emerged as the rising star in the Gambino's Connecticut operation, controlling the bulk of illegal gambling, drug, and loansharking activities in southern Connecticut.

The feds had an inside mob informant who supplied them with names and information about the drug operation and players in the Gambino crime family. Billy concocted a story that he was Manny Gibson, a New Haven drug dealer looking for a new source of supply, a potent buyer with the big-time backing to purchase narcotics. The federal informant was Billy's entree into meeting mid-level players in the cocaine operation.

He knew that generally an Italian hood lacked a traditional academic education, had been reared in the streets, and survived as much by his balls as by his brain. His social skills were weak and distrust for black Americans strong. He was intensely cynical about dealing with anyone outside of his ethnic group and had developed a street lingo for designating a black man. They called him a "moolinyan," slang for *melanzane*, the Italian word for eggplant. They also called him "tootsoon," the slang word for *tuzzone*, which in Italian translates to the color of charcoal.

Yet Billy knew that one common denominator could entice an Italian-American hood and an African-American drug buyer to get together. Whatever prejudice, fear, or hesitation Italian mafiosi felt about dealing with a black man would be dwarfed by their love for the color of his money.

If a moolinyan had money, they wanted it more than they distrusted him. That's the mindset Billy needed.

So Billy played the game. He was Manny Gibson, a big-time drug dealer from New Haven. At his sides were associates Graveyard, played by State Trooper David Osario, and Crush, played by Grayling Williams of the DEA. Billy's federal informant introduced him to Larry Zezima of Stamford, who was under investigation for delivering major shipments of cocaine from Florida to New York and Connecticut. In their first meeting at Three D's Cafe in Stamford, Zezima fronted Billy a sample of cocaine which would be followed by a sale of a larger amount if Billy liked the stuff.

"Here, take this and see if you like it," Zezima said to Billy. "It's a gift."

Billy shook his head. "No, take the money."

"No, take it as a gift," Zezima countered.

Billy stuffed five hundred dollars in Zezima's shirt pocket. "Look, man, this shit I'm buying ain't Kool-Aid," Billy told Zezima. "I ain't down here to make friends. I'm down here to make money. This is business."

It wasn't long until the federal informant passed along word that Zezima had told his drug associates about a black man with a red Porsche who was "all business."

As with all gang members Billy infiltrated, he tried to establish a common ground of conversation to bring their guard down and to create a comfort level with the target. For some it might be boats, women, cars, clothes, nightclubs, or guns. Zezima was into watches, so Billy would learn about brand names, quality, and where they originated, and engaged Zezima in conversation about them.

At one meeting, Zezima introduced Billy to one of his drug

CHASED

couriers, Paul "Rabbi" Graziano, a computer wizard who owned a consulting business in New York City that earned him six figures. In one year, Graziano's freebasing habit wiped out his bank account, submarined his business, and cost him his house and his wife. Two weeks after the meeting with Billy, one of the deputies of Broward County Sheriff's Office observed Zezima inside a Greyhound bus terminal in Fort Lauderdale carefully removing a leather bag from a taxi. He watched him put the bag on Graziano's shoulder while Graziano stood in line at the ticket counter. The deputies stepped forward and grabbed the bag. They arrested Graziano. A search of the leather bag revealed 9.5 pounds of cocaine. Graziano told police that he was paid $4,000 to deliver the cocaine to an individual at the Port Authority Bus Terminal in New York City. He agreed to assist the Broward County Sheriff's Office and the Drug Enforcement Administration in making a controlled delivery of the cocaine.

Two weeks later, when Graziano arrived at the Port Authority Bus Terminal, he was met by Zezima and another male, Vincent DiPreta. All three men were arrested when they attempted to leave the bus terminal.

Shortly after, Billy and Special Agent Grayling Williams of the DEA met with Zezima at the Five Star Video Store in Stamford, a business operated by Zezima. During the meeting Zezima said, "Look, unfortunately, because of my arrest in Florida, I can't handle the stuff myself." He promised to introduce Billy to one of his associates, John "Pasta" Progano. A few minutes later Zezima picked up the phone and told Progano to bring seven grams of cocaine to the store. Later that day, Billy and Agent Williams met Progano in the parking lot of the Stamford Motor Inn. Progano sold the agents 124.3 grams of cocaine.

They found out that the key drug supplier in the operation was one of Anthony Megale's boys, Richard "Bam" Terico, already facing state drug charges and therefore cautious about doing business with the heat turned up.

Getting to him would not be easy.

Because Terico was in a cooling-off period, underlings were not eager to hook him up with new drug contacts. On three occasions Billy visited one of Terico's favorite hangouts, the 19th Hole in Stamford, hopeful that he might run into him there. He didn't. Each time, Billy left his beeper number with a red-haired waitress.

"Please make sure he gets this number," Billy said to her. Each time Billy slipped her $50 for delivery. After the third trip to the 19th Hole and $150 in tips, Billy scored a birdie. Terico called him on his pager.

"Who are you and what do you want?" Terico asked curtly.

Billy tried to act low key and friendly. "I'd really like to come visit you to talk about some business."

Terico wasn't buying. "What business?"

"I really think it would be better if we connected in person." Billy said, not losing his cool.

Again Terico's antennae went up. "How did you hear about me?" he added, leaving Billy no choice but to be more specific.

"I've met with Zezima. Didn't he talk to you about me? I'm from New Haven."

Zezima had passed the word about a black man from New Haven who was "all business." Terico remembered and was at least curious enough to meet with him.

Billy and Agent Williams met Terico at Howard Johnson's in Stamford. At Terico's side was one of his flunkies, Teddy Farfaglia. At the meeting Terico got right to the point. "Listen, I don't even fuck around with people unless they're prepared to buy $5,000 or more."

"Okay, give me some shit for five grand. If I can move it, I'll come back and deal with you on bigger buys," Billy told him. "If this works for me, it'll work for you."

Terico did not deal with blacks. But something about Billy's

C H A S E D

style—his calm, direct candor—provided enough of a comfort level. In the back of HoJo's, Billy gave Terico the money and Farfaglia handed Agent Williams the cocaine. As Terico and Farfaglia headed inside the hotel, Williams decided to test the drugs right on the spot. He pulled out his drug tester.

"What the fuck are you doing?" Billy screamed. "You can't be testing this shit here, in the fucking parking lot. These guys will kill us if they see us. Just wrap the shit up and let's go."

"I want to make sure it's good," Agent Williams replied.

"This shit ain't going to depreciate," Billy reasoned. "Why do you have to play Joe Fucking Scientist? Let's get out of here."

When Billy returned to the Statewide offices and weighed the drugs, he discovered the bag was seven grams short. Through informants, Billy learned that Farfaglia had a reputation for shorting buyers, so Billy sent a message that he would not tolerate this kind of transaction. He knew if he was being shorted intentionally and did not speak up, he would be considered one of two things: a fool or a cop. Terico promised to make good on the deal.

Billy felt that he had now established enough rapport with Terico to be introduced to other members of his operation, especially since Terico wanted to maintain a lower profile. Billy told him that he had the money if Terico was willing. Terico paused and looked at Billy for a long moment. "I'll hook you up with my boys," he said, for the first time lowering his guard to a black man.

CHAPTER 17

"The Boys"

"THE BOYS," AS Terico called them, were John DeFelice, a Mafia enforcer suspected in two murders, and Joseph Candito, a Gambino associate who had an arrest record starting from 1958 and ranging from assault to armed robbery. They were not two men to piss off—or piss on.

Billy and Agent Williams met with Terico, DeFelice, and Candito at Howard Johnson's in Stamford. Billy learned that Teddy Farfaglia was in hot water because he had shorted a couple of buyers on drug deals. The first thing Billy and Agent Williams did was let them know they were tapped into the drug community's information pipeline and weren't pushovers. Terico had been standing aside, letting his associates handle the deal. He stepped forward now. "What's happening, Manny?" Terico said.

"I'm no Joe Donut, don't be trying to glaze me," Billy said.

Grayling Williams introduced himself to DeFelice and Candito. "I'm Crush. How you doin'? As long as we don't have to deal with that fuckin' Teddy."

"Yeah, we don't like him," Billy added.

"He was the one that shorted us," Agent Williams added.

"Motherfucker!" DeFelice said. *"That's* what's going on. He's a gambling degenerate. He takes from fuckin' everybody. You got a scale?"

"Yeah," Billy said.

"You got a scale? Then there's no problem. You can't get short with a scale."

"You got that right," Billy said. "I got nothin' but a G-note on me now. If you can hook me up, we can hook up again."

"All they want is a couple or three ounces," Terico said. "They only have a G-note."

"Oh, come on. I don't want to break that up. I can't break that up," DeFelice whined, referring to his bag of cocaine.

Once again Billy had to think on his feet. He only had a thousand dollars on him because that's all his federal supervisors could supply him with for the buy. This was not new. On several occasions Billy was prepared for a major score, only to be told red tape was holding up approval to release the buy money. This made it difficult for Billy to portray himself as the big-bucks buyer so crucial to this investigation. He was not dealing with guys from the housing projects. These were serious, seasoned drug dealers who wanted big scores. They were smarter and more paranoid than any he had dealt with before. This was an important meeting for Billy and Agent Williams. Two black men had to prove to three connected Italian men that they were serious about doing some heavy business. If they came across as amateurs, they were screwed.

"Oh, man!" Billy responded. "We came all the way down here to establish a relationship. If you can hook us up now with just a

CHASED

little, there will be a whole lot more to come."

"Listen, you're gonna be seeing me and him, okay?" DeFelice said, pointing to Candito. "We ain't gonna be able to short you. You bring your scale every time. Like I told you, you felt uncomfortable on the phone, you don't know me. I don't blame you. I respect that. I want to do business the right way. I want you guys to be right with the weight. So there's no problem. This way you'll come back, we'll service you."

"I hear you," Billy said.

"Too many fucking rats out there," DeFelice said.

"You ain't shittin'," Grayling Williams added, his face dead serious.

"Can't you bust that up for me?" Billy asked about DeFelice's supply. "Cause I only got a G-note on me now."

"Well, if you would have told me that over the phone, I wouldn't have wasted your time," DeFelice told Billy.

"Damn!" Billy cried.

"Did you say you were shorted?" DeFelice asked. "That's what it boils down to, that motherfucker Teddy. But that's why he's gonna get his. I'm gonna cut his fuckin' fingers off his fuckin' hand. Motherfucker!"

DeFelice was about six-foot-three, 240 pounds. To Billy, he looked like the kind of guy who could snap a man's fingers with his bare hands.

"Yeah, Teddy's fuckin' bad," Candito added.

Agent Williams returned from making a phone call. Billy looked at Williams. "You call Graveyard for cash?"

Williams nodded. "He can get it together, but it's gonna take a while."

"How long?" Billy responded.

"Not till later tonight, so I told him to forget it."

"Well, what did you want, what did you guys want?" DeFelice asked.

"We only have a thousand on us," Agent Williams said.

"When you called us earlier, we had more money, you know," Billy added.

"You were nervy, I respect that," DeFelice said, "but you need more money. Do you want to set it up later tonight? Or do you wanna do it tomorrow? Very simple."

"Tomorrow would be chill," Billy asked.

"Your phone's cool to talk to, right?" DeFelice asked.

"Yeah," Billy said.

"We'll conduct business the right way," DeFelice said, "but that fuckin' Teddy guy's out. His fuckin' hands are gettin' crippled. He's no motherfuckin' good, that cocksucker. Do you guys move a lot of pot?"

"We could," Billy responded. "That shit would move."

"That's wide open all over," DeFelice said.

"Can you get me in on some of that?" Billy asked.

"We're workin' on that now," DeFelice said with a wave of his hand.

"We got bank reserves for that," Billy went on. "Weed, man, Jamaican motherfuckers usually running that up there. They keep their clientele for that shit."

"Oh, they love their fuckin' pot," Candito said.

DeFelice began to move away. "Let's pack it up for now and we'll do it tomorrow," DeFelice said. "No sense in you hangin' around."

Billy appealed to DeFelice, "Instead of wasting your time, can you hook us up with somethin'?"

"I don't want to break it," DeFelice reiterated about the cocaine. "We'll see."

"Alright, see if you can break it," Billy enthused. "That way, everything's chill, we don't leave on no bad note or nothin'."

"Ah, you guys got bad timing," DeFelice said. "I gotta go for a long drive. I gotta go."

Billy persisted. "Let us buy something."

DeFelice shook his head. "I gotta go for a long ride now. I'm gonna meet some other people, okay? I gotta go for a long ride." He paused. "You want a thousand dollars' worth?"

"Yeah." Billy's eyes lit up.

DeFelice shook his head again. "A thousand? I ain't gonna break that up."

"You have to wait until tomorrow," Terico said.

Agent Williams jumped in. "We're talkin' about buyin' you somethin' to drink."

"Okay, that's fine," DeFelice said. "I know what you were sayin' earlier that you don't wanna waste your time comin' down here. I don't blame you."

"I'm sayin' we're here, you know," Billy said peevishly.

"Another time," DeFelice said. "Once you get to know us you won't have to ride around with a fuckin' scale. We do things the right way, okay? Teddy's a gambling degenerate. He keeps fuckin' nippin' at the bag. He'll be taken care of. He can run, but he can't hide."

Billy and Williams walked away empty-handed that night. However, they didn't embarrass themselves or lose credibility with DeFelice and Candito. A week later, Billy and Agent Williams met the two men at the 19th Hole in Stamford.

"You wouldn't fuckin' believe it," DeFelice said, sniffing. He ordered a vodka martini.

"You okay?" Billy asked with a showman's instinct for conveying sympathy.

DeFelice sneezed loudly. "I think I'm getting over a cold. I'll be honest with you, I'll do anything but crack. I'll do anything but that bullshit. We got a large quantity of weed."

The conversation returned to Billy being shorted by Teddy Farfaglia. DeFelice promised to cover the shortfall.

"How much were you shorted?"

"Seven grams," Billy gestured unhappily.

"Alright. That's no big deal. Just to keep you guys quiet. He was afraid he was gonna get killed. He went to his father. He went to his wife. He went to his uncle. I went after him one time. There was a lotta people who went to the club that you gotta respect. People from New York."

"I wonder what his problem is," Agent Williams asked.

"He likes to gamble," DeFelice responded disdainfully. "People are funny. I mean, I don't know you guys. You gotta take a shot like Columbus did, right? Take a shot around the world."

"That's it," Billy said, his eyes on DeFelice's beefy face.

"You know, you gotta start taking a shot with guys. It's up to you if you're comfortable with me. If I don't take no shot with you, I don't make no money. I'm getting divorced, you know? I gotta start all over again. Next time I see you I'll have the extra seven on the side."

"Alright," Billy said.

"This fuckin' town is red hot, right? We can do business together. If you want to get heroin, we can fix that. We know people down in New York. It's a dirty fuckin' game, okay? We do business the right way. And everybody will be happy. But next time we don't meet here. We'll tell you a spot, or we'll be on the highway somewhere."

"That would be chill," Billy made the word *chill* sufficiently pointed.

DeFelice continued, friendly now. "See, I'm not a known dealer. I'm a truck driver out on disability. So I'm not a known dealer. If I don't know ya, I don't talk to ya. It's not that I don't trust you guys. I gotta take a chance to earn money. If I don't take a chance, I do nothin'. We're low key. We're unknown. We were stickup guys."

"So what's Bam gonna do?" Agent Williams asked, referring to Terico.

CHASED

The muscles around DeFelice's mouth tightened. "Bam's playin' it low fuckin' key right now," DeFelice said. "I'll be honest with you: He's goin' away. I'm tellin' ya now so you know 'cause you don't see Bam around no more. But it's no big deal. We know guys up at the prison. We'll set it up for him after he goes up there and he'll be okay. We're gonna be looking out for him, that's why we're here."

"As long as we know that you're runnin' the show," Agent Williams said.

DeFelice looked at Candito. "What's he gonna do, Joe, fifteen months? Maybe ten months. We know a guy who runs a halfway house, a good friend of ours, we could get Bam there. This guy's a big heavy-duty senator. The guy's big time now. They get guys out no matter what you are. It's who you fuckin' know today. He got ratted out by one of his partners."

"Rabbi," Billy said, referring to Paul Graziano. His eyes swung to DeFelice.

"This is my own kind," DeFelice explained. "Italians. My own fuckin' kind. You get good and bad. There's a lot of bad blacks. We know a lot of them are fuckin' rats. Just like you got bad Italians. You can't judge a book by its cover. You gotta talk to the guy, give him a fair shot. If he gives you a fair shake back, then you do business with him. That's how it works. That's how we got together with you guys. Since Bam will be going away, we can service you. I don't like doin' it, but what the fuck? Money is money, like you said."

"Can we do somethin' today?" Agent Williams asked.

"Like what?" Candito said.

"An eighth?"

DeFelice nodded. "Yeah. Pay thirty-five for an eighth. Why don't we do it right across the street. It's private."

Billy glanced briefly at Williams then turned back to DeFelice. "Right across the street?" Billy asked. "That's cool."

Increasingly, Billy and Agent Williams were getting into DeFelice and Candito, setting them up for the big takedown, while they recorded as much information they could about their operation.

The foursome met again a few weeks later. Billy and Williams knew DeFelice and Candito still were somewhat uneasy about dealing with them, and they let them know the feeling was mutual.

"What's up?" DeFelice asked.

"You tell us, man," Billy responded, his voice conveying irritation.

"What do you want me to tell ya?"

Billy wanted to put the two dealers on edge. He pressed them. "Why the third degree and shit yesterday? You had me all nervous and shit."

DeFelice flushed. "Who gave you the third degree?"

Billy met his eyes. "Both of you gave me the third degree."

"I didn't give you no third degree," DeFelice insisted.

Billy shrugged. "I'm trying to figure out if something is wrong."

DeFelice shook his head. "Bam called you, right?"

"Right."

DeFelice continued. "Something was on his mind. I guess he wanted to get it off his chest with you."

"Well, why isn't Bam here?" Agent Williams asked. "I mean, I don't understand what the fuck the problem is."

"We don't force anyone to go with one particular guy," DeFelice said.

"Yeah, well then, he would know that," Agent Williams countered sourly.

"Pretty simple," DeFelice said. "You go where you want to go. Right, Joe?"

"Sure," Candito grimaced. "He's a funny type of kid."

Williams's face got red. "He can be nervous all he wants, but he can keep that shit to himself because I don't give a fuck, you

CHASED

know? If I wanna buy a tape deck from Crazy Eddie and a CD from Sounds Alive, that's my motherfucking business!"

"There's no problem with me with anybody," DeFelice muttered. "I'm gonna let you guys know, because I told you I'd always be up front with you guys, right? Now there's something going on between Bam and this guy and the other guy and that guy. But this is all baby shit, all baby bullshit that goes on. It don't mean nothin'."

"Yeah, that's cool," Billy said, his mind still on the bug.

DeFelice broke in. "But what did I tell you before, okay? I was comfortable with you guys. I'll deal with you guys. I respect you. You ask me, I ask you. You ask me, you wanna shop. Hey, listen, you wanna shop for price. That's fine. But goddamn, that should never come back to my ears."

"I'm just trying to get the best price," Billy said. He felt like sighing but restrained himself. They stared at each other.

"Manny, we understand all that, but sometimes the cheaper price ain't the way, either," DeFelice countered. "So when we heard that, the other guy got paranoid. Can't blame him, can ya?"

Billy tried to speak more reasonably. "That was a while ago. That's the only reason that we came to you, because they didn't produce."

DeFelice regarded him curiously. "Whether it was a while ago, a year ago, it shouldn't have been brought up."

"It never even fuckin' came up," Billy grumbled.

DeFelice pacified him. "I'm not mad at you. That didn't bother me, what I heard, 'cause I ain't worried about it."

Referring to Zezima, Billy asked, "Is Larry droppin' dimes on us, or what the fuck is going on here?"

"I'm scared of him," DeFelice said, his eyes cold. "You know, I'm scared, you know? I don't want to knock him. The guy, as far as I know, the guy never did anything to me."

"Well then, Bam should come clean with us and then he should tell us if he knows something bad about Larry," Agent Williams said sharply. "If Larry's a rat. If Larry's product is no good. You know, if Larry made some kind of deal or something."

"I don't know that," DeFelice said. "See, all these guys were partners at one time. They're all cuttin' each other's throats. Alright, here's the deal, okay? I told you before, whether Bam or me and Joe you're dealing with, you were seven grams short. I got seven grams for you. I'll give you the seven grams. You do what you want. If you want anything else, it's up to you. Because I gave you my word last time, you will get the seven grams. Now me and Joe are responsible. Me and Joe are eatin' that. I want to do business the right way. I want you to feel comfortable when you're with me. Bam gets paranoid quick because he can't take another pinch. What if you get pinched?"

"I ain't no rat," Agent Williams shot back.

"Well, that's good," DeFelice watched him. He flashed a brief smile. "I ain't no fucking rat, and neither is Joe. We're in the middle, we're in the fuckin' box a lot. See, there are these little kid games these guys play. Joe's almost fifty. I'm forty-something years old. We're not fuckin' kids. Them fuckin' other guys I don't give a fuck about what they do. They don't put nothing in my pocket. Like I told you before, the Italians are the worst. They're very jealous fuckin' people."

Candito broke in. "Can you give them the seven things? Because I'm gonna take off."

DeFelice's usual cocky self-assurance resurged. "I'm gonna give it to them. I'll take care of it," DeFelice said.

CHAPTER 18

Who Killed Tommy DeBrizzi?

On March 24, 1988, Billy and Terri Boone of Statewide met with one of the key players in the cocaine connection, John "Pasta" Progano, at Five Star Video in Stamford.

"I'm getting married in a couple of weeks," Progano told the disguised undercovers. "If you need cocaine while I'm away on my honeymoon, call Robert Romano."

Larry Zezima was throwing Progano a stag party the next evening.

"Hey, Larry told me to stop by your party," Billy said. "He said to get the tickets from you."

"Yeah, come on by, it'll be a good time," said Progano, who handed over three tickets. Billy smiled wryly, thinking of the strange joke—a black man was being invited to a Mafia stag party. What a goof.

The next evening, Billy got out of his car at the Stamford Community Center flanked by his two bodyguards, Graveyard and Crush. The parking lot was filled with Cadillacs, Mercedes, and BMWs with Connecticut and New York plates. Inside, the room was packed with two hundred white males. Some dressed in slick black suits, open collars, and glitter hanging from their necks; others had the Guido look—beer bellies hanging out of polyester suits, smoke from their cheap stogies fogging the buffet line.

In the background, a deejay played Italian ballads by Jimmy Roselli and Jerry Vale sprinkled with Italian dance music. Guests hit the buffet table, which featured sausage and peppers, baked ziti, manicotti, stuffed eggplant, chicken cacciatore. Guests sipped white wine, red wine, highballs, and cognac. Throughout the smoke-filled room, men with high-flying gestures discussed low-down deals.

Billy looked around the room and then over his shoulder at Graveyard and Crush. A part of him wanted to be back doing deals in the ghetto.

"Damn," Billy whispered, "I know we don't belong in this motherfucking place."

Billy stood tall, six-foot-four, playing his role of the black leader of a New Haven–based drug operation to the hilt. At his side were Graveyard and Crush, both black, pokerfaced, and thick—six-foot-three, 230 pounds—in business suits. Grayling Williams was new to the Drug Enforcement Administration. David Osario was new to Statewide. Before his assignment there, he had been a road trooper, a "pavement jockey," for the State Police. But for these purposes, they fit the role—mean and nasty-looking guardians of a narcotics king with money to spend.

As the three entered the hall, everyone looked up and stopped

CHASED

talking. Their mouths open, their eyes wide with amazement, they watched three black dudes walking into an Italian stag party.

"Who the fuck invited these guys!" muttered a chorus of men, swallowing hard.

Just about everyone in the room knew everybody, except these three black guys. Billy turned to his bodyguards and whispered half-jokingly, "Hey, if any shit goes down, it's every man for himself."

Looking around, Billy noticed one separate table of about eight guys, obviously a select group of men because the others went over to say hello, pay their respects, and express their gratitude for being allowed within talking range. These were the boys from New York. Holding court at this table was Anthony Megale, along with members of John Gotti's crew who had driven up from New York.

The feds waited, staked outside, noting the comings and goings of vehicles with New York plates. And as usual, Billy wore a wire that evening. The feds also had their confidential informant in the room, the man who provided them with updates on how Billy was being received by Terico, DeFelice, Candito, and the others. Billy was earning high marks.

As the men in the crowded room returned to their drinks and conversation, Larry Zezima welcomed Billy and his pals to the stag. While they exchanged pleasantries, Billy watched from the corner of his eye as friends of Pasta Progano handed Zezima huge wads of money and thick envelopes stuffed with cash. It seemed rather bizarre to Billy. However, he later found out it was an old Italian custom. The man who throws the stag collects the money for the groom-to-be. One by one, men forked over gifts of cash to Zezima, who later handed over probably something in the five-figure range to a happy Progano.

Zezima brought Billy around the room to meet some new faces. Downstairs, away from the main gathering, men played craps, blackjack, and poker. Then Billy ran into a couple of familiar faces,

John DeFelice and Joe Candito, whom he had not seen for about eight weeks.

Shortly after Billy's last meeting with the two men, Thomas DeBrizzi's frozen, bullet-riddled body had been discovered in the trunk of a car at the Trumbull Shopping Park. DeFelice and Candito disappeared right around the time of the DeBrizzi hit. The FBI facetiously told Billy this was oddly coincidental.

"Hey, you guys have been out of touch," Billy said, sipping the drink he carried.

DeFelice nodded. "Yeah, things were a little hot, so we went away for a few weeks. But we're back now. I'd like to move some pot. You interested?"

"I can't fuck with it unless it's big weight," Billy said, finishing the drink and putting it down on a nearby table.

"How about a hundred pounds?" DeFelice fingered his own drink. "I have it down in Florida. Why don't you come down and pick it up?"

Billy glanced over DeFelice's shoulder to see who was watching them. "I won't go down myself. A friend has a plane. I'll make arrangements with him."

After the stag, the feds asked Billy to find out some information about the DeBrizzi murder. The FBI speculated that John Gotti sanctioned the DeBrizzi hit to make room for Anthony Megale and that DeFelice and Candito were involved.

Billy kept going over the request in his mind, wondering how to approach two mobsters about a mob hit. He decided to set up a meeting at an Italian restaurant in Stamford. Billy did not want to jump into the topic right away for fear of making them suspicious. He planned to spend some time in idle chatter and move in cautiously.

But Grayling Williams was not in a cautious mood.

"Hey, do you know anything about the DeBrizzi hit? We could use those guys," the DEA agent blurted out.

CHASED

DeFelice and Candito froze. They stared first at Billy and then at Williams. Billy felt the sweat from his armpits trickle down to his ribs. He had to think fast and respond calmly, for fear DeFelice might reach over the table, grab him by the throat, and beat some respect into him.

"I have dudes who owe me some money," Billy said matter-of-factly, trying to take the heat out of the conversation. "I might need them taken out, if you know somebody. The DeBrizzi thing was all over the news; if you guys can hook me up with the guys who did it, I'll pay big time. I have a business to run, and I need to set an example. If I continue to let this guy get away with what he's getting away with, it's going to make me look bad."

Billy ordered rum and cokes for the table. He wondered if he had come on too strong. He thought, *I sound like a Mafia don who wants to send a message.* Only he was black. The Black Mafia?

He searched the faces of his companions. They didn't appear hostile. "I want a message sent out, in front of people," Billy continued. "We don't want a local person."

There was silence in the room. DeFelice and Candito pondered Billy's proposition. Finally, DeFelice broke the ice. "We might be able to help you."

"You guys are all Italian motherfuckers. I don't know who's doing what," Billy said.

"Yeah, DeBrizzi was taking money," DeFelice said. "That's what happens. Megale's moved up. This is going to help us out. Gotti just met with Megale in Stamford."

"It had to be a sanctioned hit," Candito said. "DeBrizzi was a made guy, and approval had to come through Megale and then Gotti."

The conversation broke off. Billy didn't push it. His case against DeFelice and Candito was too important—the investigation too fragile—to allow an unsolved mob hit to distract it. He didn't learn for sure about DeBrizzi's assassins, nor was it paramount.

He'd pass along the information to the feds, happy to leave the restaurant alive. He left the DeBrizzi thing alone—just another file in the mob morgue of unsolved murders.

CHAPTER 19

The Setup

BILLY HAD SUCCEEDED in winning DeFelice's confidence and arranging a series of smaller buys. Now, he decided, was the time for a big deal. He arranged a two-kilo deal—with a street value of half a million dollars—at a McDonald's parking lot just off I-95 in Darien, Connecticut. On a warm September afternoon in 1988, Billy and Agent Williams hopped into DeFelice's car.

"Hey, you got the money?" DeFelice asked, holding more than two kilos of cocaine wrapped in a plastic bag bearing the words "Just Say No To Drugs."

"Yeah, my boy over there driving that Z has the money," Billy said.

DeFelice tensed. "Hey, you guys aren't trying to set me up, are you?"

"No, man, everything is cool. I'll sit here with you until he brings the money."

Agent Williams jumped out of the car as though he was fetching the money and removed his hat. It was the agreed-on signal. The federal agents moved in. As the feds converged on the vehicle, DeFelice stomped on the gas and the car shot off. The force of the getaway jerked Billy's body back. His head bounced off the window. DeFelice accelerated the wrong way on I-95. Grabbing onto the steering wheel with his hands, Billy stretched out his foot to reach the brake pedal. DeFelice was as thick as a wine barrel, not an easy man to overwhelm.

"Motherfucker!" DeFelice shrieked. "You set me up. Motherfuckers!"

Cars and trucks zoomed toward them like torpedoes. "Stop the fucking car!" Billy yelled, kicking at the brake, fighting the wheel, and dodging honking cars screeching by at 60 miles per hour. Billy's heart was pounding.

In desperation, he pulled out his gun and stuck it in DeFelice's ear.

"You're all through, motherfucker!" Billy yelled, pressing up against the big man. "Stop this motherfucking car or I'm going to kill you!" Adrenaline surged through Billy's body.

DeFelice got the message. He pulled the car to the side of the highway and stopped. The feds in pursuit were right behind. "Okay, you got me," DeFelice said, raising his hands as he exited the car.

"Fuck you, you motherfucker. You ain't shit," Agent Williams shouted at DeFelice. "You guinea motherfuckers think you run everything. Fuck you, Mafia shit."

"Why the fuck do you have to piss this guy off?" Billy said to his partner. "We got the guy, why rub it in?"

Furious, DeFelice stared at Billy and Grayling Williams. His face was red, his eyes bulging. He had bought into Billy and Grayling's act and had been taken. Worse yet, they were black.

CHASED

Extending his index and pinky fingers toward the two undercovers, he cast an Italian curse on them. "What's happened to me will happen to you. Someday things will even out." He was cuffed and hauled away.

Billy looked at Grayling Williams. "Why the fuck did you have to break this guy's balls?"

"Don't worry about it. He ain't shit," Williams fired back.

Billy knew there was no time to waste. Immediately after the DeFelice bust, a one-kilo buy was set up with Pasta Progano and Robert Romano at a Stamford shopping center parking lot. Billy and Williams made the exchange with Progano and Romano. As soon as Billy announced the hit signal, "fresh package," Williams grabbed Progano, but Romano slipped away. As Billy tackled Romano from behind, his gun fell out of his pants. The two men rolled about the parking lot fighting for the gun. Federal agents rushed to Billy's side. They restrained Romano and made the arrest.

Billy's investigation led to a federal grand jury indictment of eight men—Richard Terico, John DeFelice, Joseph Candito, Larry Zezima, Pasta Progano, Robert Romano, Thomas Pierro, and Teddy Farfaglia—on a variety of drug charges. All were sentenced to at least six years in prison.

On June 9, 1989, Assistant U.S. Attorney Dennis King wrote the following letter to Sergeant John Petrowski of the Statewide Narcotics Task Force.

Dear John:

Now that all of the defendants have been sentenced in *United States v. Richard Terico, et al.,* and *United States v. Laurence Zezima, et al.,* I wanted to write to you concerning the performance of Officer William Chase.

As you know, Officer Chase was operating undercover during these investigations, posing as a drug dealer from New Haven, Connecticut. His convincing portrayal resulted in the infiltration of two of the largest drug conspiracy rings in Fairfield County, Connecticut. Officer Chase's testimony during the trial of Joseph Candito and Thomas Pierro amply displayed the professional attitude he continually demonstrates in the performance of his duties. Finally, Officer Chase's ability to work effectively with federal and local law enforcement agencies has, in my view, greatly contributed to this office's ability to successfully prosecute major narcotics offenders in lower Fairfield County.

Simultaneously, during the narcotics investigation, Billy assisted the feds on a separate wide-ranging investigation of Anthony Megale's criminal enterprise, an investigation that included racketeering, illegal gambling, and extortion.

Milo Dowling, one of the FBI's top Mafia experts, asked Billy to work in a gambling angle to the Megale investigation.

Of all the pushers he dealt with in the cocaine connection, Billy had the easiest exchanges with the dark-haired, good-looking Zezima, who seemed always to have answers for everything. It was Zezima who had invited Billy to Pasta Progano's stag party. Billy learned that he could discuss anything with Zezima as long as spending money was part of the conversation. One afternoon at Zezima's video store, he complained to Zezima about not having a reliable source to place his sports bets.

"I have some money to bet," Billy told Zezima, "but I don't have a contact I can trust."

"I can help you with that," Zezima said.

"Do you know anyone handling some action?"

"No problem," Zezima beamed. "I got you covered. Call these people and tell them I told you to call."

Zezima wrote down a Stamford phone number on a piece of paper. Billy turned the number over to Milo Dowling. The phone number Billy delivered scored a remarkable coup: a court-

CHASED

authorized phonetap revealed a giant illegal sports betting operation that extended from southern Connecticut to New York City and included football, basketball, hockey, and horse races. It was operated by the Gambino crime family.

After hundreds of hours of surveillance and massive federal raids in Stamford, Connecticut, and New Rochelle, Port Chester, and the Bronx, New York, undercover agents seized records that revealed the interstate bookmaking operation collected fifty million dollars in wagers annually. It was a mob-profit bounty beyond expectation.

December 7, 1989, was indeed a day of infamy for Anthony Megale. That day the man John Gotti installed as the head of the Gambino crime family's Connecticut operation was arrested with twenty-one members of his crew on charges of racketeering, illegal gambling, and extortion.

U.S. Attorney Stanley Twardy, who worked closely with Billy on nailing Mariano Sanchez and the Number One Family, called the roundup the "dismantling of the Gambino family hierarchy and operations in Connecticut."

The indictment said that Megale supervised and operated illegal gambling businesses in southern Connecticut and Westchester County, New York. But for whom? As Megale and his boys pleaded guilty one by one, the feds were using the Megale investigation to build a case against John Gotti.

Gotti was making the government look bad. He had beaten them three times before. The public's appetite for knowing more, reading more, hearing more, and watching more about the most celebrated mobster since Al Capone, the leader of La Cosa Nostra, fueled the ambition of media-hogging lawmen. But as with most mobsters who took on an air of invincibility, Gotti's loose tongue would be his undoing. Time and again he talked into a bug the feds had secretly planted in a Little Italy social club in Manhattan.

About one year after the Megale roundup, the feds charged

Gotti with murder, tax evasion, and racketeering. Billy's investigation led to one of the racketeering counts against him, which detailed a criminal enterprise that stretched into Connecticut and included a huge sports betting operation run by Megale and controlled by Gotti.

Gotti encountered another problem: His most trusted hand, Salvatore "Sammy The Bull" Gravano, one of the most feared Mafia killers ever to take the oath of silence, turned rat in exchange for a reduced prison sentence. Gravano told the world everything—details of the Castellano hit, Gotti's empire, who ran what, who had made the Frank Piccolo hit in Bridgeport, everything.

On April 2, 1992, a jury of seven women and five men pronounced John Gotti guilty of charges ranging from murder to tax evasion to racketeering. He'll likely spend the rest of his life in prison.

It was a day of celebration for Billy Chase, who had ventured where no black undercover had gone before, infiltrating members and associates of the Gambino crime family.

"I was like Indiana Jones," Billy said. "It was an adventure. The case allowed me to exercise my imagination, my knowledge, and put it all together to make it work. There were no short cuts and no easy ways to reach my goal. It was a job."

CHAPTER 20

The Color of Law Enforcement

"THESE MOB GUYS won't ever expect a black guy to be a fed," said the informant in the Gambino crime family case. "They only know the white feds."

Billy also believed that the color of his skin would immunize him from the suspicion of mobsters skilled in skunking out a cop. Still, while his race was an asset on the surface, Billy's success was directly tied to his ability to transcend the Italian hoods' utter contempt for dealing with a black man.

Yes, he knew being black diverted attention from his undercover job, but he also knew just as easily it could have gotten him killed. Could he overcome the distrust, the fear, and the bigotry? As one of them, John DeFelice, told him, "I don't like it, but sometimes you have to take a chance."

DeFelice took that chance because Billy put him at ease and massaged his comfort level. Only the most skilled observer of human nature, greed, and power could have pulled it off, and Billy qualified as an expert in all three areas.

Billy's color was clearly an asset when he infiltrated black drug dealers. No one played the part, looked the part, or talked the part better than he did. Many of his investigations were brought against non-black drug dealers working in conjunction with predominately white law enforcement agencies—cases such as Dr. Miller and Ty Williams, the Gambino crime family, and Colombian drug groups. And each time, Billy's skills transcended race.

However, being black was more a liability than an asset. The difficulties caused by Billy's skin color often manifested themselves in the most basic ways. For example, he worked closely with a number of federal prosecutors who brought cases against drug dealers based upon the details of Billy's investigations. There were times Billy was so removed from the general population that not only was he undercover, he was underground. Support staff in the U.S. Attorney's office may have heard of him, but often they did not know what he looked like.

Unlike the freedom of white undercover agents working for agencies such as the FBI and DEA, Billy could not walk into the U.S. Attorney's office without being stopped by the secretary at the front desk.

Billy dressed as though he was undercover all the time—flashy, like a drug dealer. Silk shirts, designer pants, two-hundred-dollar sneakers, an earring adorning his lobe, and a beeper attached to his belt were his uniform.

"Hi, I'm Billy Chase. I'm here to see Stan Twardy," he'd say to the secretary.

CHASED

"Is this about your case?" the secretary would ask.

"Yes, I'm here to see him about a case."

"When were you arrested?" she'd ask, thumbing through paperwork, looking for his name, thinking he showed up to work out a plea bargain, as so many others were.

"I wasn't arrested. I'm not here for the reason you're thinking. Could you please just tell Mr. Twardy Bill Chase is here."

This became a routine conversation for Billy, and each time Twardy, or one of his assistants who needed to see Billy, would emerge from his office with a big smile and warm greeting. The curious staff would wonder and murmur about the snazzy-looking black guy who looked like a drug dealer.

Black undercovers were uncommon in the federal agencies that Billy worked for. If Bill Hutton, Dave Cotton, Dale Seymour, or, for that matter, lesser known white federal agents had official business in the U.S. Attorney's office, they were never confronted by staff asking them when they had been arrested. Billy didn't get that same respect. To avoid interrogation, he had to identify himself as Officer Chase.

Many of Billy's cases brought him into wealthy suburban communities in Connecticut such as Westport and Greenwich, where he exchanged and provided information with local police departments whose members were almost always white. When he worked undercover cases of any kind, Billy routinely entered police stations from the rear of the building as a means to limit exposure to people who might be connected with one of his investigations: suspects, friends of suspects, cops who tip off suspects, or lawyers.

One afternoon, he knocked on the door at the rear of the Westport Police Department and presented himself. Flashing his police ID, Billy politely asked the uniformed cop to open the door.

"Go to the front door," the officer said.

"I'm a cop. I'm working on a case with you guys," Billy responded.

"Who are you with?"

"I'm with Statewide Narcotics."

"Why are you coming back here?"

"I'm working on a case with your department, it's sensitive, and I don't want to risk being seen by someone."

"You'll be okay. Go to the front."

White cops who worked for Statewide regularly entered the rear of the Westport Police Station; however, unless Billy knew who was on duty in the Westport PD and had asked to be let in the rear door, he met with resistance. Eventually he called the police station from his car phone to notify officials he would be entering from the rear.

He received the same treatment in Greenwich. He was constantly trying to overcome the prejudices of white members of law enforcement agencies unaccustomed to working with a black man. Most of Billy's cases were highly specialized and far beyond the expertise of local police departments. Most often, when local law enforcement had a major drug problem in their towns, they called the more seasoned and better equipped state and federal agencies for assistance, which engaged Billy's skills. Even when the people of their communities were benefiting from his expertise, Billy was often judged first by color; his skills came second.

Some cops were subtle about it, but others were more direct.

"Some white cops would not share information—even the most basic information like names, addresses, and telephone numbers," Billy says. "They acted like I was not their equivalent."

"White cops didn't like Billy because he sidestepped everybody and went right into undercover work," says Officer Ron Bailey, a friend of Billy's from the Bridgeport PD. "I'd always hear the rumblings from jealous cops who wanted to do the ultimate work. They'd always say, 'What makes Chase so special?' Billy was special because he did things no one else could do. He was made for undercover work."

CHASED

Billy never squawked openly about bias—no militant ravings. He'd reach out to his white cop friends to secure information for him, or had no choice but to work through the lack of cooperation. His sense of identity and the results of his work did his talking.

"Billy did things both white and black cops said couldn't be done," says Bailey. "They said he couldn't do Colombians and Jamaicans; he did them. They said he could not do Mafia guys; he did them, too. After a while they realized it wasn't about color. His skills got the job done. When he pulled off these cases, it was like the miracle of the day."

Billy was also grappling with the constant psychological burdens associated with the profession. Deep covers like Billy live in a fantasy world outside of the mainstream. They're asked to carry out the role their playing, living on the edge of very exciting, fast-paced, glamorous assignments, pulling down the highs of a con artist. He was never grounded in the organization in which he worked —no training programs, stress management therapy, or debriefing sessions.

An undercover is often divorced from the support of his family, but he is dependent on the contact person who is monitoring him. In Billy's case, because of his color, he was often estranged from the only people who could have supported him. No one looked for warnings or symptoms of stress, or provided the kind of caring and tending that deep covers require.

No one—least of all Billy himself—thought his obsessive commitment to duty and the loneliness that being a black undercover provoked would catch up to him. But eventually, it did.

CHAPTER 21

Death Notices

FOR BILLY, THE FALL of 1989 was bittersweet. DeFelice, Candito, and company were in prison; Megale and his crew were under indictment, and prison cells were being readied for twenty members and associates of the Gambino crime family. Though Billy had accomplished some of his highest goals, he never took the time to enjoy the results of his work.

Instead, as always, he had a new target in mind.

Julio Padilla was a drug dealer who had made himself infamous as the leader of the Young Lords, a Latino youth gang that rose to prominence in the 1970s. In recent times he had used a gas station in Bridgeport as cover for a massive drug operation. Drug buyers loved to see Padilla. If their drug purchases were large enough, he would send them off with a full tank of gas on the house.

Billy began to make a few visits to Padilla's gas station, where he engaged Padilla in small talk, filled up his tank, and turned Padilla into a friendly acquaintance.

One afternoon, while filling his gas tank, Billy dug his hand deep into his pants pocket and pulled out a wad of cash. Thumbing through the hundreds and fifties for a twenty to pay Padilla, Billy gently leaned on his gas-attendant friend for advice. "You know, I was supposed to get hooked up, but this dude I've been dealing with isn't very reliable," Billy said, holding the stash of cash in front of Padilla's eager eyes. "I wish I could run into someone more consistent."

"I can help you," Padilla said.

"You can?"

"No problem. Here's my number, you give me a call and we'll take care of you."

Billy nodded, accepted the phone number, and later made contact with Padilla. A few days afterwards, he visited the station. Inside, Billy made an ounce buy of cocaine and arranged for future buys. One of them was to take place at Padilla's Bridgeport home. Around seven that Thursday, Billy walked into the house and was introduced to Padilla's dark-haired, petite wife, Tori. Looking at her elfin face, Billy realized he knew the woman as Tori Santana. They had attended Central High School together.

Billy felt beads of sweat forming on his forehead. Most of Billy's classmates had lost track of him after high school. Once he entered law enforcement, Billy had disappeared from the social scene, and class reunions and gatherings with old school chums were not on his agenda. Nevertheless, Billy always felt uneasy about investigations that involved former schoolmates. There was always the possibility that someone knew he was a cop. Working in his hometown made the odds even greater.

This time he saw the flash of recognition in Tori's eyes. "Oh Billy, how have you been?" Tori said to him. "What have you been

CHASED

doing with yourself?"

Billy didn't lose his cool. "Ah, you know, I've been around," Billy said. "Things okay with you?"

"Sure, me and Julio are doing fine. And you?" she asked smiling.

He breathed a sigh of relief. It was obvious from her friendly attitude she didn't know anything about his real career. It was another narrow escape.

Several weeks after Billy made a buy at Padilla's house, federal agents arrested Padilla for drug trafficking. As a result of the disclosure of evidence at court proceedings, Padilla and Tori learned that Billy Chase was the undercover who broke up their drug operation. Tori did not take the news lightly, and this time she knew where he was.

The Bureau of Alcohol, Tobacco, and Firearms was one of several federal agencies for which Billy worked. ATF is an agency of the U.S. Treasury Department, and its case load primarily involves illegal transportation and sale of guns, liquor, and tobacco products—and bombings.

If Billy encountered a drug case that involved the sale of weapons, he worked under the supervision of ATF. On other occasions, ATF agents would bring Billy in on a weapons case that involved drug trafficking.

While Julio Padilla was in prison, ATF was conducting a separate investigation of an illegal weapons operation that included Tori Santana, who was busy pricing automatic weapons. Unbeknownst to her, the person she had contacted was a federal undercover agent, Ted Weaver.

During her meeting with Ted, Tori angrily began denouncing the cop who had caused her husband so many problems.

"Look, I want this cop done," she told the undercover. "I'll pay ten thousand bucks to get him killed."

"Who do you want done?" Ted asked.

"His name is Billy Chase. He busted my old man. I want him dead. Can you do it?"

"Let me check it out. I'll get back to you," Ted coolly replied.

When John Petrowski of Statewide told Billy about Tori's plot to kill him, Billy feigned emotional pain. "You mean to tell me I'm only worth ten thousand dollars?" he said to Petrowski in mock disbelief. "She was only going to pay this guy ten grand to hit me? That's all I'm worth. Damn."

Not long afterward, Tori was arrested on federal weapons charges and conspiracy to murder a police officer.

Billy shrugged off Tori's threat; no serious drug undercover could expect a threat-free career. Billy wasn't in law enforcement to make friends. But he wasn't in it to be killed, either. And after Tori Santana's plot was uncovered, death threats and attempts on his life came at a rapid-fire pace.

One evening, while dining at the American Steakhouse in Bridgeport, Billy was greeted by the sound of the alarm blaring from his car. When he rushed outside he found both doors wide open and the rear tires punctured. Two witnesses said they saw a man enter the car with a bag under his arm. When the alarm set off, the man fled.

"It looked like someone was trying to put something in your car," one of the witnesses told Billy. Instantly Billy thought about the Dicks brothers. They had bomb specialists who gleefully blew up cars. This time he found nothing; they were playing cat and mouse with him.

Federal prosecutor Holly Fitzsimmons urged Billy to leave town while investigators fanned their intelligence network for clues.

"Just get out of town for a little while," Fitzsimmons told Billy. "Let things cool off for a while."

Billy resisted. "I don't have time to bleed. I don't have time to die," he said. "All I have is time to get my work done and complete

CHASED

my cases."

"Don't take this shit lightly," Paul Salute, who headed the DEA office in Bridgeport, told Billy. "I knew an agent who was doing undercover work in Thailand. They said he was going to be killed. Instead they killed his family."

So Billy chilled out for a few days in New York City. When he returned, not only did the threats continue, they intensified. Stronger messages and outright attempts on his life plagued him. One evening he found himself face down on the floor of his living room, ducking bullets fired from a passing car. Things were so hot now that even some of his cop friends, such as Ron Henderson, were afraid to get near him.

Further aggravating the problem, both mothers of his children sent out standing orders: "Stay away from my son." Billy cherished his children and avoided anything that would pose potential harm, but not seeing his children at all—not being part of their lives— hurt him intensely.

He found himself becoming paranoid as he tried to narrow down the field of suspects who wanted him dead. The Dickses? Some were in prison, some were out. Mariano Sanchez was in jail, but who among his following wanted to get even? Frankie Estrada was in prison, too, but the Terminators didn't have their name for nothing. John DeFelice and Joe Candito were in prison, but the racketeering roundup of Anthony Megale's crew was underway. Increasingly, mob guys were becoming as familiar with Billy Chase as with the white undercovers they knew. How many Jamaicans, how many Colombians, how many Dominican dealers were slowly finding out that Billy wasn't really Manny Gibson, the big-time drug dealer, or some other alias by which he was known? Or how about classmates he lunched with at Central High School who now were rotting in prison?

Maybe it was one of the many little guys he put away, some easily forgotten psycho jailed for a year over a hundred-dollar bag of coke and who would like nothing better than to make a name for himself. It isn't just the dealer selling the weight who burns with the motivation and the mission to do a cop.

Billy had shut down multi-million-dollar drug rings. His investigations led to more than one thousand arrests. His airtight cases led to a 100 percent conviction rate. No one Billy Chase arrested ever squeezed out because of a technicality, a faulty piece of evidence, or a rights violation. When Billy Chase did dealers, they were done. Now they wanted to do the same thing to him.

"Billy Chase was one of the best cops I ever knew," says Joseph Walsh, the retired police chief of Bridgeport, whose law enforcement career spanned nearly fifty years. "He was probably too good. When you take away five years of someone's life, they don't forget easily."

In the streets, Officers Ron Bailey, Anthony Brown, and Earl King heard from informants that "they're going to do Chase. Major dealers want him."

Bailey pressed informants for names. He got the same vague answers. "Major dealers."

"They're too scared to give up names," Bailey said.

"The word on the street was, Billy was bagging everybody he played basketball with in high school," says James Ruane, a criminal defense attorney who represented a number of Billy's arrests. "Billy was dangerous because he was so effective on the witness stand. He was more effective than any DEA agent."

One afternoon, Billy walked across Reservoir Avenue in Bridgeport, heading to the liquor store. A BMW with New York plates zoomed by. Poking his head out of the car window a black man shouted, "We know who you are! It's just a matter of time!"

Billy had seen neither the car nor the man before.

Weeks later, Billy's car was stopped at a red light at the corner of Main and Capitol Avenue, one of the busiest intersections of the city. Billy looked in his rearview mirror and saw a BMW roaring

CHASED

down on the tail of his Audi. The car skidded sideways behind Billy's car. In his mirror he saw the driver drop his right hand under the steering wheel, as if he was reaching for a weapon.

"Oh, shit!" Billy shouted. He reached for his gun, but he wasn't packing. It was one of the few times he had left it at the house.

In a quick burst, he stomped on the gas pedal and screeched off. The BMW pursued. Billy sliced his car through a series of side streets, searching for the BMW in his rearview mirror, praying he had lost his pursuers. He had.

Billy raced back to his home and quickly let himself in. Sweat was pouring down his face. Wiping it away with a trembling hand, Billy immediately called Roger Falcone, his supervisor in the Bridgeport Police Department. "Who was it?" Roger asked anxiously. There was no answer. Billy hadn't a clue who it was. He felt as if it was open season, and he was the prey. Kill Chase, win a prize. His world was becoming more maddening by the day.

CHAPTER 22

Torture

BILLY HEARD POUNDING on his living room door. It was late—after midnight—and the thumping startled him.

"C'mon, Billy, open the door," a deep voice boomed in the night. From the living room, Billy approached the door carefully. He turned the knob, cracked open the door, and peeked through the narrow opening. Recognizing his visitors, he swung the door open. Staring at him with stoic faces were the members of his unit in the Bridgeport Police Department: his supervisor, Roger Falcone; his friends Ralph Villegas and Frank Pisanelli; and several others, many of whom he had worked with since his first day on the job in Bridgeport.

"We have a warrant, Billy," Falcone said to him abruptly.

"Do you want me to serve the warrant?" Billy replied with shaken voice.

"No, we have to serve this warrant ourselves."

"What for?"

"We're serving it on you! It's a warrant to search your house."

"My house! What for?" Billy asked, astonished.

The police unit barged into Billy's house. They turned over and tore through everything in sight. Nothing was left untouched.

"What is this?" Billy shouted in disbelief.

The search turned up a bag of cocaine, the very bag Billy had confiscated from a drug dealer that day. Falcone held the bag in his hand.

"What the fuck is going on!" Billy screamed.

"Billy, you're under arrest," Falcone snapped. "You're coming with us."

"Billy, you're being set up," Villegas jumped in. "The mob hired them to set you up, to take you out of the picture."

The intruding cops pulled their guns. Billy pulled his. Villegas jumped to Billy's side. A wild shootout pitted Billy and Villegas against the rest of the members in his division. In a frenzy, automatic weapons turned the inside of his house into a war zone. Then Billy's gun jammed. He pulled and pulled on the trigger but it would not budge.

Billy watched helplessly as a bullet ripped open Villegas's chest. Three others blew apart his abdomen. Blood began to cover the torso of Billy's fallen comrade.

"Run! Get the fuck out of here, Billy!" Villegas called from the floor, the wounds draining his life.

Outmanned and outgunned, Billy crashed through the window of his living room. He burst into the street and sprinted in the direction of the Bridgeport police station. Gripping his gun, running with the fury of a hunted man, he reached the front of the courthouse near City Hall. Police cars screaming in the night pulled alongside

CHASED

of him. Cops jumped out of their cars, their weapons poised. Then they fired point-blank. Billy saw a muzzle flash like a bolt of lightning cursing a gloomy sky.

He screamed. He opened his eyes, and sat straight up. He looked around him. He was in bed, terrified. The sheets on his bed were drenched with perspiration. His night clothes were soaked. Sweat poured down his face. His heart pounded triple time.

As he awoke from the nightmare, Billy's emotional state hit meltdown. He crumpled up in the corner of his bedroom, pulled his legs tightly to his chest, and dropped his head to his knees. The overwhelming pain and torture of isolation brought him to his lowest point. He wept until he could cry no more and then lay on his back, wondering what was next.

As the threats against his life mounted, Billy suffered the ceaseless torture of nightmares almost every night. The punishing images were savage. In one dream, Billy beat a man so badly his hand lodged inside the man's skull. When Billy lifted himself off the floor, the man stood up and they continued to fight, his skull in shattered pieces.

In another, Billy gouged a drug dealer's eyes out—he saw only two black empty holes—yet the man fought on. In still another, he beat his brother to death with his fists. Billy would wake up searching for open wounds and blood on his hands.

Every place where he was shot in his dreams was an area where he had suffered an on-the-job injury: where he had been bitten, he was shot; where he had hurt his shoulder, he was shot; where he had been cut, he was shot; where he had injured his neck, he was shot.

The dreams were so horrific that he wouldn't allow himself to sleep. He drank pot after pot of coffee, took No-Doze, and spent long nights in front of the television set until the dawn broke.

He was also consuming potent pain killers for an assortment of injuries. "I'm walking around like a zombie," he vented at his girlfriend Lillian Wells, who was at his side during many of the nightmares, offering comfort from the horror.

"Billy used to wake up in cold sweats, sometimes screaming," Lillian recalls. "The dreams had me so scared. He wouldn't tell me too much about the dreams, though. He couldn't talk about them. I did my best to provide as much emotional support as possible, but it became evident that the support he needed I couldn't give."

The threats and the nightmares made Billy think he was going crazy.

Just as in his dreams, his real-life tragedies continued. He lost his friend John Ramik to leukemia. The day after Ramik died, Billy dreamed that Ramik walked into Billy's house wearing a State Police uniform. Ramik handed him a nickel-plated .357 magnum. Billy fired the weapon at a drug dealer and saved his own life. This was the first time in a dream that his gun had worked.

"During this time, when he came to visit me at work he always wore dark glasses," Lillian said. "He didn't want to be near crowds. I used to ask him to take his glasses off because I didn't want people to think I was going out with a mobster."

Billy's once low-key precautions became full-blown paranoia. Anyone who knocked on his door was met with a gun in the face. When he walked into a restaurant, he insisted on sitting at a table facing the door. He refused to go to places like shopping malls, anywhere filled with people. Fearful questions crowded his mind. Where were his enemies? Who could emerge from the crowd with a gun?

One day, as Billy was dining at a favorite restaurant twenty miles from Bridgeport—where Billy always felt relatively safe—a white man, his hands buried in his jacket pockets, strode toward Billy.

Billy saw the man advancing. In a split second he tightened up and fingered his gun.

"Aren't you Billy Chase?" the man asked.

"Who's asking?" Billy snapped back. "Take your fucking hands

CHASED

out of your pockets!"

Shaken up by Billy's response, the man replied, "Don't you remember me?"

"Fuck no. I've never seen you in my life." Billy pulled out his gun. Patrons scattered, screaming with fear. They ducked for cover.

The man looked dumbfounded. "Hey, we went to St. Augustine's School. We were in the fourth grade together. Remember our teacher, Miss Dubay?"

Taking a deep breath, Billy relaxed and laid his gun on the table. He did not remember his schoolmate, but never could he forget St. Augustine's and the teacher. "I'm sorry," Billy said, both relieved and embarrassed.

"Okay, so maybe you don't remember me. Is that any way to treat somebody?"

Billy was apologetic.

"I'm sorry, if only you knew the kind of work I'm in, you might understand. I'm a police officer . . . "

"You're nuts," the man said, shaking his head. "Good-bye." He walked out of the restaurant without looking back.

CHAPTER 23

Train Wreck

JUNE 1990. ORLANDO JIMINEZ was a crack user and crack dealer who had an outstanding warrant with his name on it. From time to time, as if Billy didn't have enough work of his own, he would help clear up the warrant-swollen files of law enforcement agencies. Now he offered to round up Jiminez and take him into custody.

Billy knew just where to look. Bridgeport's historic Washington Park, the first park donated to the city by P. T. Barnum, was the location of a Latino festival. Drug interlopers in increasing numbers had forced many of the decent people out of the beautiful tree-lined park.

But on this early summer day, Washington Park was loaded with Latinos celebrating their heritage with music, dance, food, and drink. Billy drove around the park, turned down a side street, and walked up the block back to the park. Milling through the festive crowd, Billy spotted Orlando holding court with a bunch of friends. He had an iced beer in one hand and a twelve-inch adjustable wrench in the other, as if he was taking a break from performing mechanical work on a car. Billy walked up and tapped him on the shoulder.

"Orlando, how ya doing?" Orlando looked at Billy and smiled like a crocodile. "Orlando, I have good news and bad news. The good news is I'm gonna let you finish your beer. The bad news is you're coming with me."

"What do you mean?" Orlando asked.

"Hey, brother, I have a warrant for your arrest," he paused. "You gotta go, you gotta go," Billy crooned as if the refrain were lyrics from a popular song.

Orlando's friends started fidgeting. Billy put his hand under his shirt, to let them know he had a gun. He flashed a badge.

"C'mon, don't arrest me today," Orlando pleaded. Billy did not want to arrest Orlando in front of his beered-up friends, in front of a celebrating crowd, in the middle of a public park. Under the circumstances, he did not want to do anything that could encourage resistance or incite a riot. Billy had to nudge Orlando away from the crowd.

"Okay, Orlando, let's go around the block and we'll talk."

They walked down the street to Crescent Avenue. "C'mon, Orlando, let's not fuck around. I have this warrant for you."

"You don't have to do this today. Why don't you forget about it?"

Billy knew that it would not be long before Orlando started running out of excuses. Orlando had the look of flight.

"Orlando, I have to take you in," Billy said.

Orlando was pumped up on crack. He was feeling mighty—and unaccommodating. Billy moved in.

CHASED

"Help! Help!" Orlando screamed to passing cars and pedestrians. "He's robbing me."

Then Billy saw Orlando take out the silver wrench he had hidden behind him. The metal caught the sunlight, half blinding Billy. Instantaneously, Orlando tightened his grip on the wrench, swung his arm forward, and mashed Billy's injured right shoulder. Billy's body recoiled. Fighting back, Billy grabbed Orlando and kneed him in the crotch. Orlando went down but quickly sprung back to his feet. Billy kneed him a second time, then a third time. Orlando took the blows to the groin as if they were meaningless pats to the face.

Relentlessly, Orlando fought back. He hammered at Billy's shoulder with the wrench. Each blow further caved in Billy's shoulder and ripped away flesh from bone. Billy fought back, but he was a one-armed fighter. He was badly hurt and needed the great equalizer.

Billy knew Orlando had a deadly weapon. There was plenty of justification for Billy to pull out his gun and blow Orlando's head off. Blocking the wrench with his left hand, Billy reached into his pants with his right hand, grasping his gun. Quickly, Billy brought out his gun, preparing to swing the weapon against Orlando's head in one motion. Billy tried to jerk his arm forward. He couldn't move it. The heavy blows of the wrench against Billy's shoulder had paralyzed his arm. Billy could not lift his gun. He had only enough strength to hold it in a downward position.

Billy hated the scene. He had taken on tougher men, stronger men. Now he was being humiliated by a punk crack head.

Billy summoned all the strength he had. Another knee to Orlando's groin. Orlando answered by bringing the wrench down across Billy's body. As Billy crumpled, Orlando grabbed onto Billy's gun. With his mind, Billy reached inside his gut for the strength to hold on to the weapon. But he could feel his body disconnecting; his sagging frame leaked blood like a colander.

For the first time, Billy Chase was losing a fight.

Suddenly Orlando's hand slipped off the gun, and Billy pulled his broken body back a few steps. This was no longer a contest between good and evil. The name of the game was survival.

To play it effectively, Billy had to use his head. "Orlando, let's stop fighting and talk about this," he said breathlessly. "Maybe there isn't a warrant on you. There's no reason for us to get killed out here."

Orlando looked at Billy oddly, somewhat shocked at Billy's appeal for a truce. Billy was lucky that Orlando was coherent enough to understand him but not alert enough to remember Billy's reputation. Billy was the undercover at the top of the drug trade's most wanted list. He had cost the drug bosses too much money and too much time rotting in prisons. Billy's head carried a huge price. Orlando stared a few more seconds. Suddenly, he ran off into a building across from Washington Park. Billy was not happy that he had let a fugitive slip away, but he knew that this time he was lucky to survive. Desperately, he stumbled back to his car to call for help.

Bridgeport Police Officer Ron Bailey was in the vicinity and answered the call. He was the first to arrive on the scene. He saw a crowd of men along Washington Park, friends of Orlando Jiminez, venomously pointing their fingers at a man running limp with a gun in his hand. As Bailey edged closer, he recognized it was Billy.

Never had Billy been more relieved to see anyone. "Just in time," he whispered to Bailey. Bailey was one of Billy's best friends and one of the most skilled law enforcement fighters in the country—a tough, intense black man with a third-degree black belt in karate. His home is adorned with dozens of trophies, plaques, and certificates honoring his achievements in organized karate competitions.

If there is a fine line between genius and madness, Ron Bailey is the archetype. Drug dealers feared Bailey. To them, he was a human snowplow who cleared the roads of street-level dealers. His karate training had taught him restraint, but they knew better than to

CHASED

piss him off. If he had to, he could rip out a man's eyes with the flick of his finger.

Most of Bailey's work was street level, the day-in and day-out, in-your-face kind of vice work. Billy's work was a different story. The guys he nailed generally controlled drug operations. Bailey and Billy constantly shared information about the drug trade. Bailey was not deep enough to get to the main man of a drug operation. When he needed an expert, he'd call Billy.

If Billy was in trouble, if he needed help in a fight, Bailey was the first phone call he'd make.

"What the fuck is going on? These guys over here are going to kill you. Your cover is shot," Bailey said.

"Hi, am I glad to see you, G."

"G" was one of Billy's common salutations. Some guys say "pal," others say "buddy." Billy would say "Hey, G," which is street slang for a guy or friend. In this case, "G" was tossed affectionately at Ron Bailey, who had saved him.

"Man, I'm fucked up," Billy said wearily.

"I can see that. What the hell are you doing blowing your cover like this? These guys are going to eat you alive."

"Damn," Billy snapped, "my shoulder is hurt. You have to help me get this motherfucker!"

Billy was in a rage. For the first time, Billy and Bailey's roles were reversed. Billy was always the calm, cool, smooth one; Bailey the high-strung enforcer.

For a powerful man, Bailey's voice was surprisingly gentle. "Look, these drug dealers are going to be around for a long time. Their children are going to replace them. Calm down. We'll get this guy later."

A vein in Billy's forehead pulsed. "No. We've got to get Orlando now. I can't stop now. . . . I can't stop now." Billy, his eyes burning, repeated these words to Bailey over and over like a man possessed.

Bailey looked searchingly at Billy. As Billy spoke, the right side of his body leaned further to the right like a big oak tree struck by lightening, ready to collapse. In his right hand, Billy's gun dangled loosely, just inches off the ground.

"Give me your fucking gun," Bailey said firmly. He took Billy's gun, tossed it in his car, and locked the door. Bailey had never seen Billy like this. A crazy crack head had broken his friend's body and spirit. Bailey began to get angry. He knew what it was like to fight a crack head. Bailey, the toughest of the toughest guys in the Bridgeport PD, had required oxygen after a fight with a crack head. Even Bailey, a cop who could handle three or four men at a time, needed assistance that day.

Looking at his beaten friend, Bailey caught fire with anger. Billy was hurt and Bailey wanted to destroy the man who'd done it.

"That motherfucker!" Bailey screamed.

Bailey entered the building in hot pursuit. Billy should have stayed back, but pride took over. He had allowed Orlando Jiminez to slip away and embarrass him. Billy had never lost a prisoner before. He was prepared to do anything to get that fugitive back. Billy limped behind Bailey into the building. He followed Bailey to the first floor, where Bailey rushed toward the first door in front of him. With a kick of his mighty leg he forced the door open. Inside, a startled woman with disheveled hair, and her two children, jumped up.

"What are you doing!" the panicked woman shouted.

"I'm looking for a man!" Bailey screamed back. "The man behind me," he added, pointing to Billy, "is a police officer. The man I want hurt him badly. Did you see or hear anything?"

"I heard someone run up the stairs," she said, her voice trembling.

Bailey ran up another flight. Billy, summoning his last ounce of strength, followed. Indiscriminately, they kicked down door after door, and almost every time a woman and her children jumped up

CHASED

in fear.

"We're looking for a man. Did you see anyone?"

Each time the answer was the same. No Orlando.

Up another flight. Billy was now gasping for breath. They eyed a door.

Boom. Another apartment door kicked in. No Orlando. They spotted an open window that led to the roof of the building, a route that Orlando might have escaped through. Bailey climbed through the window and onto the roof. As he looked around, he saw that Billy, dripping blood onto the gravel, had followed him.

Bailey looked at Billy. He shook his head. "He's gone." Bailey stared at his friend's face. It was battered. Billy cradled his bleeding shoulder with one bruised, swollen arm. "We're going back to the car. I'm taking you to the hospital," Bailey said firmly.

Billy nodded, not speaking. He despised his own weakness, his shoulder carved up and caved in, blood dripping on his sneakers and reddening the rooftop.

A short while later, a massive law enforcement team consisting of State Police, FBI, DEA, and a dog search unit, arrived at Washington Park for a massive manhunt. Orlando slipped away that day. He would be found another time.

Meanwhile, Billy and Bailey arrived at the office of Billy's orthopedic surgeon, Dr. Donald Dworken. Billy collapsed in a chair.

"What is wrong with you?" Dr. Dworken said, shaking his head. "How did you do this to yourself?"

Billy didn't even try to answer.

□   □   □

In the next few weeks, Billy underwent surgery to reconstruct a badly torn shoulder. According to the doctors, the damage would keep him out of work indefinitely.

The disability drove him deeper into depression. Everything

that could possibly go wrong seemed to be happening: no more work, no more contact with his children, the women in his life also had had enough. Theresa divorced him. Mickey broke off their engagement and gave Billy the ring back. Lillian was still his friend, but she knew he needed help.

Billy's emotional extremities were becoming worse. His friends were frightened watching him. One day, Ron Bailey watched Billy light cigarette after cigarette, never stopping. Bailey could see the pressure and isolation closing in on Billy. He was drinking, smoking, babbling on the telephone incoherently. He couldn't eat or sleep.

"I want you to see a psychiatrist," Bailey told him. "You need stress management. It's time to take a break. I'm afraid you're going to eat your gun."

Jackie Flynn also pushed Billy to seek therapy. The first therapist Billy visited, psychologist Susan Monk, recommended a specialist. "I thought this stuff only happened on Miami Vice," she told him. Monk sent Billy to Carl Rotenberg, head of the psychiatric unit at Bridgeport Hospital.

Rotenberg summed up Billy's condition: "This is like being in Vietnam after the war is over."

Billy entered Park City Hospital for rest and treatment, both emotionally and physically.

Even after he got out, nothing seemed to be going right. His string of bad luck continued. On the evening before he was scheduled to have the sutures removed from his ailing shoulder, he was at home. He heard loud voices in the street below and looked out his window.

Three teenagers were trying to steal his car. Billy ran outside and grabbed the biggest of the bunch as the other two fled. Billy pulled out his cuffs with his left hand and held the beefy teen with his right hand. Resisting the cuffs, the boy forced his arm away, jerking Billy's injured shoulder. Billy heard a sound like a rag

CHASED

being torn in half. He collapsed in agony. Oddly, the boy Billy was placing under arrest took pity on him.

"Hey, are you okay?" he asked. Billy was in no mood to be friendly. He threw the cuffs at the boy.

"Put these fucking cuffs on! Wait here."

Billy stormed into his condo and called for back-up. Not long afterward, a patrol car arrived and the teenager, having handcuffed himself to a metal railing, was arrested.

Again Billy was taken to his orthopedist and examined. Shaking his head, Dworken said, "This time your shoulder is ripped in four places, and part of your arm is held by a thread of muscle." The cortisone shots Billy had been taking had deteriorated his shoulder bone. Dworken called in a team of surgeons. Billy needed three operations to reconstruct his entire shoulder.

Afterward, Billy still held out the vain hope that his shoulder would heal and he could resume work. The doctors told him he was through.

CHAPTER 24

The Final Days

ONE MORNING IN the spring of 1992, Billy walked out his front door to find that his BMW was missing. Later that evening, police recovered the car in a city housing project. Bullet holes savaged the entire vehicle. The front and back windshields had been blown out. It looked like a coffee can that had been used for target practice.

A few days later, flipping through his mail at home while talking on the telephone with John Petrowski from Statewide, Billy came upon a piece of mail with no return address. Billy opened the envelope: "How much did it cost to get your car fixed?" the letter read. "You know who did it. It's just a matter of time. We're not going to get you first. We're going after people who are close to you. Like your girlfriend. You'll be the end result."

The letter writer signed off, "U Pig."

"You should see this damn letter," Billy said to Petrowski, his voice full of urgency. "Who the fuck are these guys?"

Billy's tormentors were a little behind the times on the subject of his girlfriend. His relationship with Lillian Wells had ended. But she was still in danger.

One morning, Lillian walked out of her home and placed her two children in her Isuzu. She got behind the wheel of the vehicle, set the car in reverse, and began backing up into the street. She pressed her foot on the brake pedal. Nothing. The car continued to roll freely into oncoming traffic. She slammed the pedal. Still nothing.

"Oh my God!" she screamed, terrified at losing control of the vehicle and the prospect that she and her children would be smashed from behind. She grabbed the emergency brake and jerked the lever up. The car halted abruptly. Breathing a sigh of relief, Lillian put the car into drive and slowly advanced into the driveway. She pulled on the emergency brake once again and shoved the car into park. Turning to her children, she yelled, "Hurry, get out!" Clutching their hands, she ran into the house.

Later, Lillian's mechanic examined the vehicle.

"The brakes are completely gone. There's nothing left," he told her.

"I can't understand it," Lillian said, perplexed. "They worked perfectly yesterday."

One week later, she walked out of the house to discover two of her car tires had been slashed.

"I kept asking myself, who's after me?" Lillian says. "Where was this coming from?"

Unfortunately, Billy knew where it was coming from, and the thought that someone close to him could be a victim was eating away at him.

A contingent of agents from Statewide and the Drug

Enforcement Administration were assigned to keep close tabs on Billy. They watched over his house and accompanied him where he traveled. But how long could this protection reasonably last? Billy was a working cop, not the President of the United States. Being constantly watched by a team of agents was not a practical solution to his problems.

A few days later, a man knocked on the door of Billy's neighbor, looking for Manny Gibson, one of the many aliases Billy had used in his undercover work, including his Mafia investigation.

"Some guy was over here looking for a Manny Gibson, you know him?" Billy's neighbor asked him. "When I asked the guy who he was, he said he was an insurance agent."

The only people who were supposed to know his aliases were members of his division. Just in case, Billy asked his insurance agent if he had been looking for him. No dice. This was getting freaky and too close. Drug dealers were playing head games with Billy. Maybe a few bent cops on a drug payroll were playing games, too.

Several of Billy's friends who worked in Patrol Division were hearing that Billy was too hot to touch, and some cops refused to back him up.

"The one-for-all-and-all-for-one stuff is bullshit," Ron Bailey told Billy. "There are some cops who are trying to burn you."

Billy discussed his situation with Bridgeport Police Chief Thomas Sweeney, who told Billy he had become too great a security risk to himself and the people around him. He was too easy to find. The Police Department already had a letter on file from Billy's psychiatrist urging his retirement and departure from the state.

"We'll retire you right away," the chief declared.

Billy's final days in Bridgeport were a tragic blur. His life had always been lived at two hundred miles per hour, too fast to offer time for introspection. Now, as he slowed down, questions abounded. Where would he live? What would he do? How could he keep his new location confidential? What would prevent drug assassins from tracking him down?

He discussed the possibility of a new identity with local, state, and federal law enforcement officials. These were supervisors who routinely provided a whole new profile for criminals, so why not a cop? They promised to do what they could once he resettled, and suggested that he do so quickly.

For the first time, Billy listened. He had to. He collected his belongings to move. Ron Bailey helped Billy load the things he was taking into a U-Haul. Throwing box after box into the storage area, Billy thought about his life.

"The bad guys are supposed to leave town," he said to Bailey, "not the cops."

Bailey shook his head sadly. There was nothing much he could add.

"Hurry, and just go," Bailey said. "Long good-byes are the worst." They embraced, not knowing when—and if—they'd see each other again. Stoically, Billy got behind the wheel and drove off. His law enforcement career was over. He left behind his children, family, friends, professional teamwork, close partners, and impeccable personnel file—and one of the most distinguished careers in the history of police work.

A State Police cruiser escorted Billy for his final journey in Connecticut. From Bridgeport, Billy drove through lower Fairfield County, past the scenes of his most remarkable law enforcement work, where he met Mariano Sanchez for the first time; past the McDonald's in Fairfield where he captured the cop-shooting fugitive Frankie Estrada, head of the Terminators; through Norwalk where he broke up a major Colombian drug ring, a group that would "never deal with a black man"; into Darien, and then Stamford, going where no black man had ever gone before, cracking part of the Gambino crime family.

Crossing the state line into New York, Billy waved good-bye to

CHASED

his escort, who returned the gesture by flashing the lights of the state car. Billy Chase was all alone now. The drive was long and seemed to take forever. As he drove, he thought about his two sons. He promised himself that he would do his best to make their family life as whole as he could. He thought about the years that had passed, all he had accomplished, all he had not. His thoughts turned to the mess his personal life was in, and he grimaced in pain. He was now playing a true version of the most dangerous game of hide-and-seek ever conceived. The hunter had become the hunted.

CHAPTER 25

Retirement

BILLY HEARD A KNOCK at his door. It had been six months since he retired from the drug wars and left Bridgeport. He lived alone in a condominium complex in a town thousands of miles away where he knew no one and people only knew him by another name. He approached the door cautiously, haunted by the memories of unwanted visitors who wanted him dead. The closet next to the front door was loaded with an arsenal of weapons, just in case. He looked through the peep hole. A sudden smile spread across his face.

"Yo, Bailey, what are you doing here! How are you, G?"

"What, did you think I couldn't find you?" Bailey said, walking through the doorway. They gave each other a high-five, then moved to embrace as they always had. Bailey noticed that Billy could barely clasp him. Billy used to squeeze him like a python. This time, he hugged Bailey with his right arm draped to his side. He couldn't lift it.

It was then Bailey realized how much Billy's injuries had sapped not only his strength but his spirit.

Bailey looked around Billy's apartment. It had the appearance of a college dorm after a fraternity party. Clothes were everywhere, nothing was in its place. The room was a mess.

This was not the Billy Chase he knew. Chase was well groomed and meticulous, as attentive to his home as he was organized in his work. Bailey spent the day cleaning Billy's house and helped prepare some meals to freeze away. Together they discussed the past and the future. Bailey, in his forties, was healthy and strong, racking up trophies and prizes at karate tournaments around the country, piling up arrests of inner-city drug dealers in Bridgeport, enjoying quality time with his children. Billy, not yet out of his thirties, was alone, depressed, unemployed—a physical and emotional wreck unable to see his children.

☐   ☐   ☐

His body still suffers from the full force of being hit by wrenches, running into concrete walls, and kicking down metal-braced doors. An inch has been shaved off the bone of his right shoulder. He has thirty-five-percent use of his right arm and a sixty-percent total bodily disability. The thoroughbred legs that had catapulted his body above basketball hoops at Sacred Heart University had lost their spring. His neck felt the residual pain of bloody fights with crack heads and free falls from drug dealers trying to kill him.

The man who once had subdued Goliaths and raced down drug dealers with the swiftness of a cheetah chasing prey now eased out of bed every morning feeling the relentless pain in the back of his

CHASED

neck, the agony of his pieced-together shoulder, the biting ache in his back, hoping the weather—and his will—would make the day bearable.

☐ ☐ ☐

A few months into his retirement, Billy took a trip on a cruise ship to get away from it all. He wanted to experience the warm sun and the cool breeze and try to think out a new beginning for himself. As he looked across the aquamarine Atlantic, a half-hour into the voyage, the winds began whipping up, sprays of water hit his face; the afternoon sun burned intensely into his skin.

As he stood there, mesmerized by the sun and wind, a shooting pain ran like needles through him. He was in agony, his legs turned into jelly and his knees buckled. In seconds, Billy collapsed on the deck of the ship. Passengers and medical personnel aboard the ship hurried to his aid.

Paramedics searched for a pulse. Nothing. They couldn't locate a beat. Applying CPR, they pressed against his chest hoping to pump life back into his heart. Startled passengers gathered around.

"C'mon, fella, respond," said one of the paramedics, feeling for a pulse.

"Do you have anything?" asked another.

"I've got something," the first paramedic breathed a sigh of relief.

Billy's heart had responded, but his body lay limp. Within a half-hour, he was lifted off the ship by a helicopter to an awaiting ambulance. He remained unconscious for another thirty minutes.

Physicians later explained that his heart had fibrillated, then stopped. On top of all his other medical problems, Billy now lives with an irregular heart beat. Medically, his heart condition is treatable, but the best medicine for Billy is the kind that can't be prescribed. It is peace of mind.

Slowly, ever so slowly, Billy tries to come to grips with his present life, understanding that the whirlwind days of one of the greatest careers in law enforcement has ended. With acceptance comes the realization that it isn't even the excitement but the little things in life he misses—playing basketball, lifting weights, jogging, swimming, tossing a football without worrying about aggravating his shoulder injury.

More than anything else, he misses his two sons. He cannot see them. He can only talk to them on a regular basis by telephone, hoping for the day he can see their faces and be a real father to them again.

Billy reads many pages a day from the Bible and spends time in prayer and meditation, as he did growing up in a religious family. His Bible study provides him faith, belief, and optimism. His faith guides him through the toughest days and helps bring an acceptance of life—its good and bad times.

"I wanted to make a mark, to contribute to society, to help people. The work I did was the ultimate work I could do, and I'm very glad I had the opportunity, although sometimes I feel like I was a government experiment, a test tube in a lab, a secret weapon never before launched. We need training programs for undercovers, we need to provide them with stress management so that they can deal with the manipulation, the threats, the everyday dangers of the job."

Billy knows the dangers are not over. There's still the possibility he could be called to testify at drug trials that are pending, or those that come up on appeal. There are also the people he imprisoned who have long memories and are back out on the streets, or will be shortly.

Ron Bailey still hears from informants about drug dealers who want to find Chase, and about bad cops who have been asked to help find him. Many of the drug dealers do not believe the reports that Billy has retired. They think he's still on an assignment somewhere, preparing to take down yet another drug operation.

CHASED

Billy knows that other drug undercovers have fallen recently. In June 1993, Newark Police Detective John Sczyrek, an undercover narcotics officer, was shot to death while waiting to testify at a trial. Day by day drug dealers grow more ruthless, more dangerous, more brutal than ever before.

In an effort to help preserve his sanity and safety, Billy reached out to his former law enforcement supervisors, asking for the help they once promised in creating for him a new profile and a new beginning.

It was a reasonable request from a marked man who still faces constant and unknown dangers. He asked for a new identity, new name, new Social Security number, new driver's license. But the only help he's received so far is some words of advice from Bridgeport Police Chief Thomas Sweeney.

"If a guy wants to get lost, you just go to it," Sweeney says. "Criminals do it all the time. Billy has to carry on with his life. The work he did was outstanding, but the fact is Billy's not working anymore."

The advice is little comfort, but the Bridgeport Police Department has no program in place that addresses the needs of undercover cops who have to retire and are on the run from the very dealers the government wants in prison. Agents such as Billy have no standing, even though threats against their lives persist because of their high profile.

On the other hand, if Billy had been a criminal with information to put others in prison, he'd have the government's forthright attention and protection, a new name, new identity, new license, new Social Security number, and financial assistance with entry in the Witness Protection Program. The government spends millions of dollars each year protecting criminals with the information to put others in prison.

Billy faces a double standard.

"Don't worry about it. These guys will forget about you," he

229

was told by various city, state, and federal officials he worked for. Yet when the cameras were on them and government officials played to an eager press, they said, "these guys" were murderous menaces to society who should spend the rest of their days in prison but were still free to commit crimes.

"I often try to figure it out, but I can't," Billy said. "Sometimes I feel like a criminal."

Jackie Flynn, who works for the office of the Fairfield County's State Attorney, called Billy the victim of a governmental breakdown that provides protection for criminals but not retired cops on the lam from drug assassins. In Billy's case, a one-man vanguard who was the best undercover of his time.

"Chase has paid a hell of a price for what he accomplished, and now he's out there on his own," Flynn says.

"He received very little appreciation for doing the best work," says Billy Perez.

"No supervisor ever looked after Billy when he was doing these cases," Bailey says. "He did cases no other cop—local, state, or federal—could do. He should have been provided stress management after each and every case. They pushed and pushed that kid until he burned. And now they have turned their backs on him."

However, Billy Chase knows in many ways he has made the difference he once dreamed of, and not only by ridding the streets of some of its worst drug pushers. Since Billy's retirement, a whole set of procedures in the training and selection of undercovers has taken shape in law enforcement—including mandatory stress management, the testing of personality factors, the caring and tending of agents, and looking for stress warning symptoms when debriefing is required to ensure that harm isn't being done to the agent.

Law enforcement is now studying the psychological dynamics of the field: the casualties of undercover officers, alienation factors that officers experience living a lifestyle outside of the mainstream, the specter of paranoia looming over them.

"We're learning a great deal," says Chief Sweeney. "In undercover work, you're playing with people's lives, subjugating them to a new role. You have to look at the danger systems, the impact on their life. No case is worth losing a life."

Billy has not given up hope that he too can live a new life—a life of peace and time with his sons and family. Lately he has been thinking about going to law school. As always, he believes he can make a difference.

Despite these hopes, Billy is aware that for the present he must continue to live a guarded life. Someone out there may be watching, waiting to get him.

He understands that his dreams of a new beginning are for the future. For now, Billy Chase is still alone and undercover.